MW01258179

Heavenly Father's

Angels:

The Ultimate Missionary Guide

by

Marcus Sheridan

BONNEVILLE BOOKS™
Springville, Utah

ISBN: 1-55517-567-8
v.1

Published by Bonneville Books
Imprint of Cedar Fort Inc.
www.cedarfort.com

Distributed by:

Typeset by Virginia Reeder
Cover design by Adam Ford
Cover design © 2001 by Lyle Mortimer

Printed in the United States of America
10 9 8 7 6 5 4 3 2 1

Printed on acid-free paper

Library of Congress Cataloging-in-Publication Data
>
> Sheridan, Marcus.
> Heavenly father's angels : the ultimate missionary guide / by Marcus
> Sheridan.
> p. cm.
> ISBN 1-55517-567-8 (pbk. : alk. paper)
> 1. Church of Jesus Christ of Latter-day Saints--Missions. I. Title.
> BX8661 .S545 2001
> 266'.9332--dc21
>   2001003917

Dedication

To my children.

I hope your missions will alter and change
your lives as much as mine has.

Acknowledgments

A special thanks to Thomas and Cheryl Lyon, and Elders Haven, Balls, Orellana, Rockwood, Degraff, Erickson, Stock, Clark, Smith, Burton, Probst, Airmet, and Lopez.

I must also thank Damon Larsen and Trent Garrett.

I also want to thank my incredible wife Nikki, who, through her example, has made every thought of this book possible.

Table of Contents

Introduction:
There is more to life than Hot Chocolate

I believe in the idea that everyone in this life, at one time or another, is put in situations by Heavenly Father which are meant to open his spiritual eyes and thrust him in a direction which can eventually lead him back to our Heavenly Father. Some people have these experiences and just dismiss them as if they had no importance. Others, on the other hand, are willing to assume the responsibility of these experiences, therefore taking a positive turn in the road of life. Perhaps you have had such an experience.

I had one during the winter of 1996. I had been a member of The Church of Jesus Christ of Latter-day Saints for a little over a year. As a senior in high school, I had been baptized mainly because of the influence of my best friend. I can remember well what a member of the stake presidency said to me shortly after my baptism. "You'll make a good missionary," he said. I squawked at the idea of such a statement, thinking the man was rather silly for even having mentioned it.

Just getting to the point of baptism had been hard enough for me. My family was already upset with my new lifestyle, some of my friends had alienated me, and to top it all off, I was getting ready to embark on my college education at West Virginia University. The idea of leaving school for two years seemed mind boggling and unrealistic. To be quite honest, I wanted no part of it. As I left home for college and the new life that awaited me, the farthest thing from my mind was a mission.

This particular winter was quite cold and snowy. As a freshman in college, I had been lucky enough to stay in my uncle's townhouse instead of the dorms. It was a very nice two-story edifice, with a deck on the second level. I spent the majority of my free time the first semester relaxing next to the fireplace in that luxurious townhouse, enjoying the cozy heat that was always prevalent, while I sprawled on the couch and played video games. Yes, I thought that I was living it up. I was in the dream pad and all of my friends, needless to say, wanted to hang out at my place.

One day, a day that set the tone for the rest of my life, I found myself doing the norm, playing video games on the couch while I slowly sipped away at a steaming cup of hot chocolate. I can recall that it was one of the coldest days of the year. I'm not sure if you are familiar with the winters in Northern West Virginia, but I assure you that they can be rather unpleasant. As I sat on the couch, relishing in my luxury and just kicking back, I looked through the sliding glass door that was on the second floor and watched the snow blow furiously outside. It must have been about twenty degrees below zero with the wind so strong that it would make tears stream from your eyes. Clearly, it was not a good day to be outside. I can remember thinking to myself that if there was anyone working outside that day, they had to be nuts.

Just about the time those thoughts crossed my mind, I heard the doorbell sound. I thought, "What kind of fool would be traveling on a day like this?" I opened the door and was surprised to find my two friends, Elder Stevens and Elder Tuck, standing there wrapped up in what must have been about five layers of clothing. They looked rather hilarious, actually, with their mismatched scarves and caps coated in snow, and teeth that chattered together like bells on Christmas. The three of us had become pretty good friends since I had been attending the student branch where they were currently working.

I told the two elders that they were crazy for being outside in such weather and that they needed to come in and warm up with some hot chocolate so that they could thaw out a little bit. The young men obliged to sit down for a minute, but Elder Stevens seemed to be perturbed about something. He looked a little fidgety, and so I figured that the weather had just got to him a little bit. I asked him what was wrong and he said that he "needed" to teach a first discussion. I laughed and told him that he was a little off his rocker for wanting to do such a thing and that what he really needed to do was just kick back and relax in front of the fire for a minute.

Despite my comments, Elder Stevens was determined. He was rather emphatic about teaching this discussion. I was confused as to why or how he could be so driven. What was his motivating factor? What gave him the desire to be outside in a blizzard when the rest of West Virginia was next to the heat of their fireplaces? Eventually, I would learn the answer to these questions.

Elder Stevens' "need" to teach a first discussion was more than just a simple whim or desire. It was a clear yearning and burning within his heart, and he was not about to let some extremely cold and miserable weather impede his goal. Nor was he about to let a warm fireplace, hot chocolate, and video games throw him for a loop. For this reason, after about five minutes of anxiety and a few sips of hot chocolate, the Elders were out the door. I could not believe the enthusiasm that these two young men had to teach a simple discussion.

From the sliding glass door on the second floor, I could see the two Elders begin their journey again. Now, as the reader, I would like you to imagine the scene that I am describing to you. Pretend that you are in my shoes, looking out that sliding glass door at those two missionaries. As they began to walk down the parking lot that was in front of the townhouse, Elder Stevens gave a slight grin to his companion and then suddenly burst into a run down the snow-covered hill that was my parking lot. About fifteen feet into his run, he threw on the brakes and slid another ten feet. With my face glued to the sliding glass door, I watched with profound excitement and amusement as Elder Stevens, after ending his slide, looked back at his chubby companion and smiled, almost nodding him on to attempt the same.

Elder Tuck followed his companion's lead and broke into a run. He looked like a wild buffalo running down my parking lot. At the end of his run, he, too, broke into a slide, but weight and gravity took over. He slid much farther than his companion. The two Elders looked at each other and shared a laugh, and then proceeded to run and slide all the way down the parking lot until they were out of my sight. I leaned against that sliding glass door for the next few minutes, unable to shake what I had just witnessed. The images of those two young men were still racing through my head.

In that moment of contemplation, the fireplace, video games, and hot chocolate seemed to have much less significance than before. Through the actions and enthusiasm of these two elders, I realized very clearly that missionary work is one of the greatest ways that we can feel a sense of happiness and accomplishment in this life. I also learned that earthly luxuries do not give us any type of eternal satisfaction.

Elder Stevens and Elder Tuck had no idea they had changed my life that day. Such was not their goal. They were just doing something they loved. They had a fire. They had grit. They were willing to pay the price. As the elders disappeared from my view that snowy, blustery day, I knew that I had an important calling and responsibility to assume. I was to be a missionary, a representative of Jesus Christ. I could no longer deny what I already knew.

Today, as I write about this simple experience four years later, that special, life-defining moment almost seems like a dream. I wish I could better describe to you what I saw that day and how I felt, but I cannot. All I know is that I will always have an image of two elders laughing and sliding their way into the sunset of a West Virginia parking lot.

What does this book offer you?

As I said earlier, I am a convert of the Church and I served as a missionary in the Chile, Osorno mission from 1997 to 1999. Needless to say, my mission was a great experience.

This is why I have written this book. I know that every missionary has the potential to have two incredible life-changing years while out in the mission field. I read a few mission prep books before I left to the Missionary Training Center, but upon reflecting on my own experiences, I wish I had known many more ways to help me maximize my calling. This book consists of many ideas, tips, and suggestions that can make a dramatic difference in any missionary's success. Some of its thoughts are common, and others are quite original. Keeping an open mind and heart, I know that you will be enlightened and strengthened.

I have also written this book as though I am talking to the young man or woman who is preparing to enter the MTC. I have only used "elder" in my writings in order to keep from writing "elder and sister," as well as "his or her" every time. This book is just as applicable to all of the wonderful future sister missionaries out there as it is to the future elders.

I believe, through my own experiences as well as the experiences of many other missionaries, that everything I have written in this book to be true. I love the gospel and the fact that I am a member of the Lord's church. I am so grateful for the outstanding and energetic missionaries that taught me the gospel, and I am grateful for all of the members out there who leave all that they have in order to reap the harvest. My mission is the foundation of my life and the essence of my being, and for all of you future missionaries out there, I pray that you will soon be able to say the same.

Chapter One:

Enthusiasm, Enthusiasm, and Enthusiasm

A merry heart doeth good like a medicine: but a broken spirit drieth the bones (Proverbs 17:22).

If there was one key to being a successful person and missionary, I believe that it would be the ability to have and show enthusiasm at all times. You must have passion in order to be successful. Be passionate about who you are, whom you represent, and where you are going. For all of you future Spanish missionaries, such passion and enthusiasm is called "animo," and it is a very powerful word! We live in an exciting time. We have a prophet here on earth who communes with Jehovah. The church has been restored to its original state; the priesthood powers are again abundant, temples are popping up all over the world, and last but not least, the Savior will soon come again. Wow! I could just go on and on about the many blessings that you and I have in these latter days. Instead of moping about all of the bad in the world we can jump for joy as we count our many blessings in this dispensation. Life is great!

Now I want you to play along with me for one minute. Think of a person who lifts your spirits or puts a smile on your face every time you're around that person. What are the qualities of this person? What does this person do to make you feel so good whenever he is around?

Take a few seconds and really answer these questions in your mind. I would be willing to bet that the person you have thought of always has a smile on his face and is always just a little more excited than the rest of the gang. Does he wake up each and every morning with such a demeanor? I would venture to say that such would not be the case, but somehow he continues day after day with this same wonderful attitude. How is this consistency accomplished? Ten keys to consistency of enthusiasm will be discussed further on in the chapter.

In every mission, there are various types of missionary enthusiasm. It is impossible to completely classify these types, but to keep it basic, I'll just give three very general classifications; missionaries type "A," "B," and "C." The "A" missionaries are those who are excited and "pumped" all the time. Such missionaries rarely (if ever) complain about counsel given from the mission president or other church leaders and are usually the first to volunteer when help or sacrifice is needed. They are also the ones who make the zone and district meetings fun, due to their energy for whatever is being taught. They have the knack for remembering to shake everyone's hand, whether it is in the street, at the door, church meeting, or zone conference. Smiles almost always radiate from their faces. They walk a little bit faster than everyone else and have a bit of a "pop" in their steps. And more than anything else, other people raise their own energy levels when missionary "A's" are around.

This is why they are so respected by their peers in the mission field. I'm sure you have already realized that these missionaries usually baptize more than others in the rest of the mission. Needless to say, these missionaries are not "fence sitters." Better yet, they are "go-getters." They set very high goals and demand more from themselves that anyone else possibly could, including the mission president.

A type "B" missionary doesn't normally have the fire like an "A" missionary, but he does get the sparks flying every once in a while, especially when he has the example of others. Such a missionary does take initiative at times and performs most duties asked of him. His goals are usually not very high but he does feel the need to reach or at least come near his set standards. "B" missionaries make up the largest portion of the mission and are counted on to perform many responsibilities.

A type "C" missionary seems to just be there for the ride. Most often, he doesn't show much emotion and if he does, he is usually complaining about someone or something. "C" missionaries tend to be the ones who get sick the most. They participate very little in meetings and are aggravated by having to give their weekly numbers reports to their district and zone leaders. Members usually aren't uplifted by the visits of "C" missionaries because they talk very little and they don't bring a better spirit to the house of the members or non-members, mainly because they tend to spend too much time in their own houses. In fact, some will even tell the members of all the problems that they are having, such as getting dogged by investigators or relaying how sleepy they are because of their strenuous work schedule. I would now ask you, as the reader, to put yourself in the shoes of a member who hears such complaints from a missionary. Would you want your friends to be taught by this elder or sister? Would you be excited to give referrals to such a missionary knowing the lethargic attitude of this individual? I think not.

Actually, there are many more types of missionaries that you will meet and serve with while out in the mission field, but the basic concepts are the same in most cases. But, what would happen if every missionary was an "A" missionary? Do *you* desire to have such fire and influence? Now is the time to set such a goal and standard for yourself.

The Book of Mormon gives us many great examples of just how important it is to have enthusiasm for missionary work. Let's take a look at the example of Alma the younger and Ammon:

"O that I were an angel, and could have the wish of mine heart, that I might go forth and speak with the trump of God, with a voice to shake the earth, and cry repentance unto every people!

Yea, I would declare unto every soul, as with the voice of thunder, repentance and the plan of redemption, that they should repent and come unto our God, that there might not be more sorrow upon all the face of the earth" (Alma 29:1, 2).

Is it just me, or does Alma seem ready to explode with energy in these two verses? He had such a great desire to serve and he desired only the greatest blessings possible. Like Alma, we must act as if we were a trump of God in our missions.

I love the example that Ammon gives us in the Book of Mormon. We have all read and studied the chapter when Ammon glories in the Lord, but I would like to look at his words in another light. Ammon states:

"I do not boast in my own strength, nor in my own wisdom; but behold, my joy is full, yea, my heart is brim with joy, and I will rejoice in my God.

Yea, I know that I am nothing as to my strength I am weak; therefore I will not boast of myself, but I will boast of my God, for in his strength I can do all things; yea, behold, many mighty miracles we have wrought in this land, for which we will praise his name forever" (Alma 26:11, 12).

The interesting thing about this story is that Ammon got rebuked by his brother Aaron immediately after he expressed his joy. Why was this? Many missionaries have had great success with respect to converting many people to Christ just as Ammon had done. Like Ammon, as a missionary has success in his mission through complete obedience, faith, and diligent work, a joy will come over that missionary and a fire will burn within his whole being. This is just one amazing aspect of bringing people unto Christ. Ammon was able to see the potential that he had through the help of Heavenly Father and he was simply stating his utter joy for what had come to pass. His joy brought a rebuke from his brother, but such can be the case at times in the mission field. When a missionary is excited and fired-up just as Ammon was, it is possible that other missionaries may discourage him. This is okay because these same missionaries will understand why such appropriate joy is shown once they have tasted success for themselves. Now, I am not saying that one should act inappropriately, but it is okay to have constant enthusiasm. Thrusting in your sickle brings so much joy; great is the satisfaction that you will feel if you do your part to build the kingdom of our Lord and Savior here on earth.

As we can see, having enthusiasm and being cheerful is a critical aspect of being a great missionary. Section 123 of the Doctrine and Covenants tells us:

> "Therefore, dearly beloved brethren, let us cheerfully do all things that lie in our power, and then may we stand still, with the utmost assurance, to see the salvation of God, and for his arm to be revealed."

This scripture is great! The admonishment is so true! Let us be cheerful and do all that is in our power and we will then see just how much of the harvest that we can reap.

Some missionaries are always enthusiastic and others just can't seem to ever get their engines started. These enthusiastic missionaries are much like that person I asked you to think of earlier. They always build up the people around them and they just seem to get excited about the smallest things. Is this an easy attribute to have? I believe that the amazing attribute of constant enthusiasm can only come through hard work and constant effort. I will now discuss some of the many things that you can do as a missionary and as a person to acquire this quality.

A Missionary's Ten Keys to Constant Enthusiasm

1. *Complete obedience to mission rules and the mission president.* The Spirit is what keeps us enthusiastic while we are on our missions. If one does not have the influence of the Spirit, he cannot stay happy or content for much time. Look at this equation for me:

Obedience= having the spirit= "fired-upness"

It is a very basic equation, but also it is a very basic truth. Also, your mission president is your guiding light for the next two years. You will find that if you are negative towards him whether directly or indirectly, you will immediately lose the influence of the Holy Ghost.

2. *Reading the scriptures and studying diligently.* For two years you have the opportunity to engulf yourself in the scriptures and other gospel studies. Never again in your life will you have so much time to do this like you do while on the mission. But if this is true, then why do so many missionaries make such terrible use of their study time? Fatigue or lack of work ethic could be a reason; nevertheless, I have always been baffled when I have seen someone blow their whole study time on non-enriching activities. I found that my studies in my mission always had a direct correlation with my overall enthu-

siasm. The scriptures and other gospel literature are meant to help you and me to feel the spirit, which will in turn make us more excited to do the will of the Father to our utmost ability, which is missionary work. Also, as we learn new information and expand our general knowledge about the Church and it's many heroes, we tend to be more and more engulfed in deep thought about these wonderful people. They then become a part of us and we can therefore feel the same powers and inspirations that they did. What a wonderful tool we have within arm's reach. I pray that we can all study in our missions with a desire to learn and apply these teachings to our important work. Let us not waste time sleeping or talking about non-pertinent information. There is no time to waste, so hurry!

3. *Prayer.* Prayer is essential to constant enthusiasm. Just as I felt so many times in my mission, you will feel completely frustrated, tired, and sad very often. In difficult times like these, it is a must that we get down on our knees and ask Heavenly Father to help us get through each trying moment with a smile. You'll be amazed as you see the difference a heartfelt prayer can make. As missionaries of the Lord's church, we have the protection and help of Heavenly Father and his many angels. They are more than ready to lend us a hand, all we have to do is reach out to them, so start reaching out today!

4. *Counsel from others.* One great aspect about missionary life is the fact that a missionary has so many wonderful people from which he can receive advise and counsel. If you ever have a problem in your mission, the mission president, his assistants, the zone leaders, and the district leaders will be there to help you in whatever way possible. It is so important to accept the fact that sometimes we

need the help. So therefore I admonish you to take advantage of your surroundings and learn to rely on the help of others whenever possible.

5. *Help from your companion.* It is an imperative to your success that you have an open line of communication with your companion. We teach in pairs for many reasons, and this is one of the main ones. It is so possible to form eternal bonds with the missionaries that you will serve with, but this will only come to pass if you both are humble enough to depend on each other and willing to sacrifice to make such a bond.

6. *Work and teach like crazy.* It is amazing the difference between the enthusiasm of those missionaries who are busy working and those that are just watching the days go by. There is something so addictive about teaching discussions to people who are thirsting for something more in this life. Once a missionary gets "lost" in his work and has a complete focus on bringing people unto Christ, all other matters become non-pertinent. The best days in my mission were those days when I would teach four, five, or even six discussions to investigators. By the end of the day my jaw would be in pain from overuse and I would be amazed at just how fast the time had gone by. Such days are every missionary's dream, and are great fuel to keep the fire burning within us as the weeks and months fly by. One other thing about work: Make it fun! If you are working hard and smart, you will soon see that it will be a "blast" for you and your companion. Eventually, it won't even feel like work, it will become a characteristic of who you are as a person.

7. *Baptize.* This one is a no-brainer. Watching someone whom you have taught enter into the waters of baptism is what it is all about. It is why we have been called by a prophet of the

Lord to take eighteen months or two years out of our lives and focus on saving souls. The more a missionary baptizes, the more joy and enthusiasm he will have. Clearly, baptism is both a cause and effect of enthusiasm.

8. *Focus.* Think about this one with me for a second. If a missionary spends all of his time thinking about his girlfriend that he left back at home, will it be easy for him to remain focused? I hope that you did not have to think for very long. It is so easy to lose the fire when a missionary is thinking about what is going on back at home. Just follow this advice: forget about your past life and get on with the one that you are now living. There is no time to let such trivial matters stand in your way and keep you from reaching your missionary potential.

9. *Exercise.* Later on I will talk more about the wonders of exercise, but just listen to me for a second on this one: elders, if you start to look like Jabba the Hutt on your missions, it is very possible that you will have his same enthusiasm as well. Eat smart and get up early to exercise. This will increase your energy levels and enthusiasm drastically.

10. *Fake it!* You are probably wondering what I mean by this, and the answer is simple: The most excited missionaries and people in the world don't wake up everyday doing somersaults with big smiles on their faces. Everyone has bad days, but the key is to wake up and do whatever it takes to get that smile and enthusiasm on your face and in your actions. This is why it is often necessary to "fake it." Smile even if you don't feel like smiling. Why? You might ask. Because after a while any fake smile will turn into a real and sincere smile. The missionaries in my mission often called me Elder Animo (enthusiasm), but just like the rest of the missionaries, I would at times feel

9

unenthused for whatever reason. I had to work to feel and look like Elder Animo, and therefore I would often start the day with a fake smile. Within a few hours my smile had turned into a true zest and enthusiasm. This may sound like corny advice, but I have a deep testimony with respect to acting fired-up even when you are not, because eventually your act will become a part of your being and you will have to put on your "act" less and less as the days go by. I would hope that all missionaries who read this would have the goal to develop themselves into uplifting people to be around because of their excitement for life as well as for the gospel!

It is possible for every person to have an enthusiastic personality day in and day out. If you are one of those people who say that you are just too calm to show much enthusiasm to your fellow missionaries or investigators, you are dearly mistaken. We all have the ability to radiate vigor and passion for this gospel; it is just that some of us have yet to develop this talent as much as others. Please do not sell yourself short. You must only expect the best. I know that you, like thousands of other missionaries, can do it. If you give heed to this counsel, I promise that you will see miracles wrought in your mission and you will be blessed beyond your imagination. I am so excited to be a member of this church and to have the complete truths of the gospel at my hands.

Like Alma the Younger, I wish that I could cry with a trump of God the good news unto all people, but I fall short in my wish, but I will always continue with the fire that I have now in saying that the gospel has been restored to its fullest and the time to act is now. There is no tomorrow when it comes to the gospel. There is only today. Let us waste no time in being the most exuberant and joyful members and missionaries that we can be!

Chapter Two:

The MTC (a.k.a. Heaven on Earth)

By this time you have received your mission call and you pretty much have everything that you need to enter into the MTC. Looking back on my preparations to leave to Provo, I would like to have brought a few more items with me. I would recommend thinking about obtaining the following items. Most of these necessities can be found in the MTC, but buying needed items is a time-consuming ordeal, and as we already know, time is of the essence.

Extra temple garments. This especially applies to those in foreign missions. Having to buy garments while out in the mission field is a hassle because it usually takes forever to receive them once ordered. You will be amazed at just how fast your garments will wear out, so be well-prepared and buy many more than you think you will need.

Colored pencils and markers. This may sound a little silly, but over an 18-month or two-year time period it is amazing just how many colored pencils you will use. I must have bought them about twenty times in my mission. You can never have too many.

More than one set of gym clothes. Do yourself and your roommates a favor (and everyone else around you, for that matter) and bring three sets of gym clothes. You will easily use them throughout your MTC and missionary experience.

A durable, thick journal for note taking. One of the dumbest things I did during my mission preparations was the fact that I did not buy a really nice journal for note taking. Please take my advice on this one and get yourself one today. During your time in the MTC, you will listen to wonderful talks and speeches every day. While out in the mission field, you will need some place to record all of the classes and talks that you give as well as those of your fellow missionaries and leaders. It is a real tragedy when missionaries take notes on those little notepads that fit in the front pocket of their shirts. We must keep and cherish the records that we have. This is difficult with some little notepad that is used up in a month's time. A nice, durable journal for note taking will be one of the best and most valued investments of your mission, as well as a spiritual souvenir for the rest of your life.

I will now talk about a few actions that every missionary needs to take before entering into the MTC.

Repentance. Hopefully, you have already taken care of this aspect of being a missionary, but if you have yet to rid yourself of past transgressions, please give heed to this counsel. If you think that you can feel like a missionary in the MTC when you have not fully repented, you need to think again. The MTC is such a holy sanctuary that all unclean things feel uncomfortable therein. The spirit is absolutely undeniable in there. Words cannot describe its holiness. Many missionaries find the need to talk with their appointed bishop once they have entered into the MTC. If a missionary has not fully washed himself from sin, this is a wonderful act of faith on the missionary's part. Most missionaries are able to repent and continue with their callings, but it is much more satisfying to the soul when one can enter into the MTC without such a heavy burden. Therefore, I give all missionaries and future missionaries a charge to repent now and free yourself from any transgression that at this moment may be eating at you from within. There is never a reason to delay this act of faith. God and his angels rejoice when we humble ourselves and wash away our iniquities.

Read over the discussions many times. The discussions are going to be some of your best friends for the next two years of your life (and beyond). They must become imbedded into your soul and mind and so it is imperative that you become familiar with the discussions right off. You will be using them everyday for the next two years, so please take the time to obtain a set and study them as if they were scripture. Since most of you will want to memorize your discussions to be the most effective missionaries that you can be, starting on them now will make them much easier to memorize quickly and efficiently.

Set your goals now! I love discussing goals so much that I am going to spend an entire chapter on their importance, but for now I will just say that it is imperative to walk into the MTC with a clear vision of what you want to get out of your mission. I know that it is impossible to set all of your goals beforehand, but many can at least be defined. Some examples of pre-mission goals would be: 100% obedience, complete respect for leadership, exercise routines, memorization time for discussions.

One problem that many missionaries have is that they set their personal goals long after they have entered the MTC, and therefore lose days, weeks, or even months of precious spiritual growth. I had this problem for the first few days in the MTC. I had a few books that I wanted to read, I wanted to memorize some scriptures, and I also wanted to learn as much Spanish as possible. As I attempted to mesh all of these things together, I found that I was getting very little accomplished. That was when I realized that I had to focus on just one, maybe two, things at a time to be as efficient and effective as possible.

It is also very important to remember, just as we will discuss later on, that a goal is not a goal unless it is written down. All great missionaries take their goals very seriously. They understand that a goal set righteously is a promise with our Heavenly Father.

Read *How to Win Friends and Influence People* by Dale Carnegie. I have never read another missionary prep book that gives this recommendation, but if you take the time to read this book, you will be amazed at just how much it prepares you to deal with people in your mission and make the most out of every relationship that you have. The most successful missionaries are masters of human relations. Carnegie is considered by many to be the country's first motivational speaker. His human-relation ideas are truly insightful and energizing. Carnegie was giving tremendous motivational talks long before Steven Covey, the great LDS author of *Seven Habits of Highly Effective People*, was even alive. Read this book. Once you have, you will understand why I have recommended it to you. It teaches the commitment pattern before it was even in existence. If you read this book and practice its principles, it will change your mission as well as your life.

Now I would like to discuss the most spiritual month or two months of your life, which will be spent at the Missionary Training Center. I am sure that you have already asked your friends who have been on missions about their MTC experiences. I would also bet that you have heard both ends of the spectrum with respect to their opinions on them. I am absolutely sure that you will only get out of the MTC what you put into it. Even today, when I think about how that place changed my life, I still can feel my chest tighten and tears come to my eyes. It tears me up inside when I hear a missionary tell me that he didn't like the MTC. To be completely honest, I can just not fathom why anyone could possibly say such a thing. Make yourself a promise that the MTC will change your life and I know that it will if you only do your part.

You have arrived at the MTC. You are probably quite nervous and confused as to exactly what is going on. Do not worry. Do yourself a big favor from the get-go and relax. You will be taken care of and everything will fall into place. The first couple of hours, maybe even days, will seem very hectic. This is only natural and before long you will be in a groove with the rest of your district.

Saying Goodbye. The time has come to say good-bye to your family and friends. This will probably be one of the more memorable moments of your life. There is nothing wrong with showing emotion. I recommend writing all of your feelings about this departure in your journal after your first day in the MTC. Although this can be a memorable and emotional experience, it needs to be short-lived. Once you have said your good-byes, it is an absolute must that you let that part of your life go and shift all of your focus on to the new life in which you are now engulfed. I know that eighteen months or two years might seem hard to fathom at this point, but just like everyone has told you, the time will fly by and soon it will feel like you have just experienced the most powerful and realistic dream of your life. Therefore, now is the time to get focused and start to think about reaching all of those personal goals that you have set. Take a deep breath and put yourself in the hands of your Father in Heaven.

Meeting your District. As you and your roommates begin to establish your home for the next month or two, you will have the great opportunity to get to know each other and begin to build a strong relationship among yourselves. The key to making this transition work for everyone in your room is the humbleness that each missionary has. In the coming weeks you will get a good idea of what it is like to live and be with someone twenty four-seven. For many missionaries, this is one of the most difficult aspects of the mission, but it need not be this way. If a missionary is willing to compromise and work every situation out, successes will almost always occur. Often, missionaries try to act like someone they are not, which in turn causes friction within companionships as well as districts. Be yourself! A very important key to forming a strong companionship, as well as district, in the MTC is to not judge anyone that you meet prematurely. Too often we form opinions of others before we have actually gotten the chance to know them. It will take quite a few days for you to even begin to know your district and your companion. The missionary who you think is serious and never cracks a smile in the first couple of days, could end up being the funniest guy you ever met as well as your best friend by the end of your MTC experience. Promise yourself now that you won't make this mistake and that you will do everything in your willpower to be in harmony with all of the missionaries in your district as well as the rest of your companions that the Lord will place you with in your mission.

The Rules. In your time in the MTC, as well as in the mission field, you will often hear missionaries complain about the number of rules that they must follow. I have seen through experience that one of the easiest ways that you and I can lose the spirit is to complain about the rules and guidelines that the Lord has given us. We must not look at rules in the sense that

they are restrictive. Better yet, we must view the rules that the
Lord gives us as opportunities to receive his many blessings.
When a missionary complains about the rules, there is a forest-
fire effect among the other missionaries. Once one person
drops the match, the blaze quickly spreads if not treated properly and can greatly damage the spirit of those who have
participated. After a few days in the MTC, I noticed that I
would sometimes complain about the many rules that I viewed
as not being pertinent. Once I realized the effect that this had
on me, I wrote down a few goals on a sheet of paper and then
laminated it. I promised myself and the Lord, in prayer, that I
would no longer complain while on my mission. Although I
cannot say that I was perfect in reaching my goal, I did greatly
improve and could therefore enjoy the presence of the Spirit
more often as I attempted to bring souls unto Christ. Let us not
be fire-starters in our missions as well as in life. If our first
reaction is to complain whenever we are asked to do something
by one of the Lord's servants, we need to seriously reflect on
our spiritual state. We must follow the example of Nephi and
react quickly to follow the directions of our Heavenly Father.
We should not take two years out of our lives to act as Laman
did when his leaders instructed him. I would also like to
admonish all future and current missionaries to write down
their goals on a sheet of paper and then laminate that paper,
and have it hanging in a spot where you can see it every day.
These goals should act as a solid foundation for you while out
in the mission field.

Class. You will probably hear the statement that "in the
MTC, the days feel like weeks and the weeks feel like days."
This statement could not be any truer. With the schedule like it
is in the MTC, the days can get really long and challenging,
physically and mentally. Physically, because you are most likely

getting up earlier than ever before in your life, and mentally, because you are attempting to cram every possible piece of information that you can into your brain in a very short amount of time. Also, since you do basically the same thing everyday in the MTC, the whole routine can seem very repetitive. Because of these conditions, it can be very difficult to maximize class time and keep focused throughout each day, everyday.

As I have said before and as I will say many more times, you will only get out of the MTC (and your mission) what you put into it. For example, you will often participate in "practices" with other missionaries in your district to simulate the actual mission field. One of the problems with these practices is the fact that they require the missionaries participating to be focused and willing to put out some effort to make the practice more life-like. Therefore, when a missionary wants to goof around during practices, nothing, and I really mean nothing, ever gets accomplished. This is why it is important to be focused in class as well as determined to get as much as possible out of each class period.

Although I am suggesting that the members of each district stay focused in class, I am also a firm believer in the idea that it is important to laugh together as a district inside and outside of the classroom setting. I was blessed to be in a district that had a very good mix of humor and seriousness. We knew when it was time to be serious, but we also knew when it was time to play. With the right mix, you will see that your district will develop quite a strong bond that has the potential to last forever. The elders and sisters in your district were chosen by God to be with you for a reason. You all have the potential to make incredible spiritual strides if you will only walk in complete obedience and cherish each other as brothers and sisters of the same Heavenly Father.

Another critical part of class is that wonderful word that we talked about earlier—*enthusiasm*. You will be able to learn the magical effects of proper enthusiasm during your stay at the MTC. Because of the demanding schedule, it is a must that the members of a district do all that is possible to keep everyone alert and excited about what is being taught.

If you are enthusiastic as well as positive about the things that are taught during class, you'll see a trickle-down affect with the rest of your district. I challenge you to always be enthusiastic while in the MTC. When doing this you will be better trained for what lies ahead in the rest of your mission and your district will be much better prepared for sharing the gospel in the mission field.

Practices. Practices are so crucial to success that I decided to stress their importance in the mission field a little more. Many elders and sisters, upon hearing the word "practice," groan at the thought of attempting to do such role-playing activities. This used to drive me nuts on my mission because I knew that practices were so helpful in making missionaries better at their callings. To be frank, it all has to do with humility. Missionaries who are humble enjoy doing practices because they understand that so many people can benefit from these exercises. Practices should be done with enthusiasm, sincere effort, and the acceptance that one can always learn from other missionaries. In the MTC, as well as in the field, I had some of my most spiritual and uplifting experiences while participating in practices with other missionaries. As missionaries, when we work together to make ourselves better at what we do, the Spirit also has the potential to bond us closer together and help us exceed the potential that we would have had if we had attempted to better ourselves alone.

Humility, as I mentioned earlier, is a needed element in

practices. If a missionary goes into a practice with the belief that he already knows all there is to know about the subject, he will undoubtedly learn nothing from that practice. Also, if a missionary is not willing to accept and analyze the feedback given to him in a practice, it is of no worth to even do the activity. We must accept the fact that we can always improve as teachers of the gospel.

There is always someone out there who can do a skill better than you and me. Unless we accept this, we will never be good leaders and we will not have the Spirit present with us when we work with other missionaries in role-playing activities. I have a strong testimony of the importance of daily practices in missionary work. I know that they can help us to be the best missionaries that we can be. I testify that we can learn from each other if we are willing to rid ourselves of pride and if our ears are open to the suggestions of others. As teachers of the gospel, the saying: "Practice makes perfect," could never be truer.

Maximizing your time as a Missionary. Every second in your mission is a valuable moment in time, and must not be treated as naught. In all frankness, "personal time" really does not exist in the mission. We must act as if every second is an opportunity to better ourselves and become closer to our Savior. Upon reading and reflecting on my own journal entries from my MTC experience, I noticed that about three or four times I wrote that I wished that the days could be thirty six hours long instead of just twenty four hours. I had so many goals and desires in the MTC that I couldn't accomplish everything in the limited amount of time I was given. No matter how much effort I put into my studies and no matter how much I learned, I always desired more. I was feasting for knowledge and my hunger could not be satisfied. Those of you who have properly set personal goals will quickly come to the realization that it is difficult to fit everything into your tight schedule. If this is not the case, and you find that you have much free time, it is likely that you're not getting out of the MTC what you could, and you are wasting the Lord's time.

As a missionary attempts to maximize his time, a complete vision and organization is needed. A missionary must learn to plan his day out and set aside time slots for all proposed goals of that day. A simple way to accomplish this is to take five minutes of every morning to write down on a sheet of paper exactly what you plan to achieve that day. Such a simple act can lead a missionary to accomplish more than he ever dreamed he possibly could. While out in the mission field, you will have to learn to be a great and efficient planner. There is no better time to begin to master this technique than in the MTC.

The Discussions. As I mentioned earlier, the six discussions are going to be your best friends for the next eighteen or twenty four months. The smartest thing that I did while in the MTC was to memorize the first discussion. For many missionaries, this would not be such a tough task if it were to be done in one's native tongue. In my case, I set the goal to memorize the first *charla* while in the MTC, despite the fact that I could not even count to ten in Spanish upon my arrival to Provo. Every extra second that I had was spent on memorizing the first discussion.

I would wake up repeating principles in my head and would go to bed reviewing in my mind what I had learned that day. I was completely engulfed in the first discussion. I found the task of memorizing the discussion extremely difficult because of my limited abilities in Spanish and also because there were many other areas of concentration that I had to work on. There even were a few times when I was tempted to just quit and wait until my arrival in the mission field to memorize the whole discussion. The thing that kept me going was the fact that I had set a goal and it was just not a personal one. It was a promise that I had made to my Heavenly Father. I knew the goal could be reached because when I had prayed about it I felt good. I just had to exercise my faith and also show a willingness to sacrifice. By the time my MTC training was over, I had completely memorized the first discussion and had even started on the second. This feat enabled me to start off much more prepared in the actual mission field because I did not need to read the first discussion as a "greenie."

Your fellow missionaries and friends may tell you that it is not important to memorize the discussions while in the MTC. To this I can only say that the missionaries who start off in the field knowing the first discussion usually are much happier because they can feel so much more comfortable while teaching, and they also are then able to memorize the rest of the discussions at a quicker rate.

I know that every elder and sister has the potential to memorize at least the first couple of principles of the first discussion in the MTC, no matter what the language is. So often the excuse, "My memory is terrible. I just can't memorize." is echoed by missionaries with respect to the discussions. If anyone has the ability to memorize a church hymn or some other song, they also have the ability to memorize the discussions. It all has to do with repetition.

Many of us have hymns imbedded in our memory because we have sung them countless times in the course of our lives. I must have gone over the first discussion hundreds of times while in the MTC, and just like the average person I struggled, but my dedication eventually paid off. This is possible with every missionary.

Learning a foreign language. This may not directly apply to those who have been called to English-speaking missions, but I'm sure that your future children who go on foreign-speaking missions will be able to use this advice. Some missionaries, upon learning another language in the MTC, stress so much about learning the language that they think they will go crazy or end up having a mental breakdown. This is not usually the case, but most missionaries that have to learn a second language while in the MTC face anxiety and fears over not being able to learn the language as fast or as well as they would like to. If you are faced with this challenge, do yourself a favor and don't stress out. As I stated at the beginning of this chapter, the MTC is almost like Heaven on earth. If such is the case, the purpose of the MTC is not to give us white hairs and cause us to lose sleep at night. As we have already learned, its purpose is to set the foundation of our missions and light the fire of our inner spiritual souls. Everyone learns new languages at different rates. I was one of those really slow learners. I would always notice that the rest of my district understood each of the rules of Spanish before I did, despite the fact that I was the most studious of the group. I did not let this get me down, though, I just kept working as hard as I could and allowed Heavenly Father to do the rest.

We must not compare our abilities with the abilities of others. We can only do what is in our power and then we have to leave the remainder in the hands of the Lord. To help you learn a foreign language, I give you these simple steps, which I have termed the *five* S's:

—Set your personal goals through communication with your Heavenly Father
—Study, study, and then study some more
—SYL (Speak Your Language)

—*Stay relaxed*
—*Stay in touch with the man upstairs*

I know that learning a foreign language is one of the most exciting and at the same time most difficult challenges that the human mind can face. It is my testimony that, just like any other obstacle that we have in our lives, Heavenly Father is willing to raise our levels of understanding to help us to overcome language barriers. I feel that, through prayer and hard work, I was quickened in understanding while in the MTC and I know that this can happen to you if you have the same focus and determination.

The Food. I have never understood why so many missionaries and ex-missionaries complain about the food in the MTC. Where else in your life will you be able to eat cereal for three meals a day? Personally, I thought the food in the MTC was awesome. Now, just like everyone else, I did have a few problems adjusting to the elements (I'm sure my roommates would testify to that fact), but after the first week or so, my body had adjusted and I felt great physically.

To many, addressing the issue of food in the MTC is not a very important or needed issue, but I believe that if an elder or sister complains about the food, it is harder for that person to feel the Spirit than for an elder who enjoys the food and rejoices over having such blessings. Often in the MTC, when I would hear a missionary complain about the food, I would say to myself, "This person is going to Colombia for two years to eat beans and rice everyday and is complaining about eating subs and crepes, what is he thinking?!" We are blessed to have such luxury in the MTC and we should learn to appreciate these blessings. Let us not complain when we have luxuries that most people in other countries could only dream of enjoying, or sometimes don't even know that such exists.

Also, it is necessary that an elder watch his diet while in the MTC. As a whole, if a person stuffs himself to maximum capacity for dinner and then tries to sit down in class for the next two or three hours, he will likely find it may be difficult to stay awake, much less sit down without exploding. Without having been in the MTC beforehand, it is difficult to appreciate what I am saying. I will just ask you to trust me and not try to see how many chilidogs you can eat every night for dinner compared to the rest of your MTC district. If this occurs and you attempt to break all of your personal eating records, you and everyone else seated next to you will be sure to dread the final class at the end of each day.

Forming a Unified District. As I mentioned earlier, it is possible that you will form eternal spiritual bonds with some of the acquaintances that you will have in the MTC. I have such a strong love for the elders and sisters that I passed two months with in Provo. We were quite a diverse bunch of people, from all parts of the United States. We also were headed to a variety of missions, unlike most districts where the elders and sisters are usually going to the same mission. Some of us were lifetime members and others were converts. Each person though, was unique in his or her own way. I have many times reflected on the incredible relationship that we shared as a district and I have tried to list the reasons as to how we were able to form such a strong bond despite our differences.

Leadership Positions. Seeking personal acclamations can do serious damage to the unity of any district. As a district, it is critical that every member is treated as an equal. Each opinion and each testimony shared by an elder or sister must be viewed in the same light as the opinion and testimony of another. Just because an elder has the calling of district leader, everyone else

25

is still responsible for maintaining a spiritual and learning environment. I think at one time or another, every member of my MTC district had to ask the rest of the class to buckle down and get on task. This helped us greatly because everyone worked to make us the best that we could be.

Eating together. As a district spends time together outside of the classroom, a friendship and love can more easily develop among the members of that district. I have many vivid memories of laughing with the rest of my district as we sat in the "east side" cafeteria and chomped away at Lucky Charms and chocolate milk.

Attending the temple together. Our district was very adamant about attending the temple together. I can vividly remember how we would all leave the temple with a great feeling of satisfaction, unity, and love for our fellow man. We also took many photos in front of the Provo temple, which was always a humorous as well as an uplifting experience.

Testimony sharing. Once you get settled into the MTC, you will see that as a district, you will have many opportunities to have group testimony-and scripture sharing. Some districts use this time to joke around, which is a shame because these sharing sessions are given to us to help our testimonies become strengthened by others as well as help us learn to communicate our feelings for the gospel and its many facets. It's amazing how a simple testimony can work spiritual miracles among different people.

The most spiritual experience that I have experienced in my life came in a testimony-sharing session with people in my district. One evening, we listened to a great talk in a fireside focused on the Book of Mormon and its power as a conversion tool. I loved the talk so much that after hearing it that evening, I headed back to my dorm room and filled the pages of my journal with the enlightening information. But my feeling of utter joy and excitement did not end there. I can remember lying in bed that night, listening to a conversation that my roommates were having. They were joking around and having a good time, but for once I had no desire to join in. I was still contemplating the magnitude of the Book of Mormon. Suddenly, an indescribable feeling came over me. My chest was tight. In fact, I felt like I could not even move my limbs. My whole body experienced a burning sensation as I lay there contemplating who I was as a missionary. It was incredible! The next morning, our district had testimony sharing. When it came time for me to talk, I could still feel the inner fire that I had felt the night before. I shared my feelings about the importance of the Book of Mormon as well as the importance of my mission. I felt the spirit so strongly as I sat in that circle with those elders, that I thought my chest would explode.

After I had poured out what was in my soul, I could see that the spirit had affected those eleven other elders so much that they all had tears in their eyes. Others joined in and shared powerful words. The spirit was so strong that it almost seemed like the Savior himself was walking among us. Personally, I honestly feel that something else was in the room with us that day. I cannot say exactly what it was, but I know that I have not since felt anything else close to its magnitude. It was almost as if we had experienced Heaven just for a minute.

Since that day, I have used that experience as the foundation of my testimony. After having felt the way I did, I could never possibly deny that the Book of Mormon is true, and therefore the fact that Joseph Smith was a prophet of the Lord. This one experience left quite a mark on our district. After that day we all could feel that we had been blessed as a group by the powers from above.

Firesides and Large Group Meetings. Firesides and large group meetings will be the highlight of your week once you are in the MTC. Each week, missionaries are blessed to hear from members of the Seventy as well as Apostles from the Quorum of the Twelve. Take advantage of these opportunities and record (in the notepad that we talked about earlier) as much information as possible. The inspired counsel that these men give you will be of great worth to you while out in the mission field.

Also, one of the great highlights of these meetings is the fact that you will sing hymns in unison with hundreds of other missionaries. During such moments of praise to our Father, the Spirit is unquenchable. Relish this experience. There will be few other times in your life when you will have the opportunity to participate in such an activity again.

Teachers. A normal schedule in the MTC consists of three classes per day taught by distinct instructors. It is important that you, as well as those in your district, remember that these teachers don't get paid very much for their services and are basically in the MTC because they have a love for sharing the gospel and they desire that every elder and sister experience success in his or her mission. Also, each teacher has a distinct teaching style, which requires that the members of each district be flexible and willing to do whatever the teacher asks of them.

Each one of my MTC instructors had a profound influence on my mission. From one I learned the importance of humility, from another I learned the importance of wearing a smile at all times, and from the other I learned how to teach the gospel naturally. I know that if a missionary desires to gain knowledge from his teachers in the MTC, he can. Just as I mentioned earlier, without humility on your part, you are assured to lose many helpful techniques and insights that could be very useful to you in the mission field. You must strive to love and respect your teachers in the MTC to the best of your abilities and I promise you that every class will be a more memorable occasion for you as well as your district.

Exercise. I find this topic so important that I will spend an entire chapter writing about it later on in the book. For this reason, I will only give a quick overview of the importance of exercise at this time. Since the MTC can seem so monotonous at times, a break in the rhythm can be a very effective method in maintaining a missionary's high enthusiasm and alertness levels. The average day in the MTC (at the time of the writing of this book) consists of a schedule something like this:

6:00 A.M.	*wake up*
6:30 A.M.	*eat*
7:30 A.M.	*sit and learn*
11:00 A.M.	*eat*
12:00 P.M.	*sit and learn*
5:00 P.M.	*eat*
7:00 P.M.	*sit and learn*
9:30 P.M.	*return to rooms and sleep*

Upon analyzing this schedule, you could probably figure out why so many missionaries gain weight while in the MTC. For this reason, and for the purpose of maintaining a high enthusiasm level, exercise is a must. Presently, the missionaries have about an hour set aside each day to exercise or do another activity of their choice. When I was in the MTC in 1997,we were only lucky enough to have three to four days a week in the gym or outside in the playing area. I found that many missionaries used this time to take a nap in their dorm rooms. I'm not going to tell you that I never took a nap, but almost every time I had the opportunity, I would participate in some form of aerobic activity. In fact, since I enjoy running so much, I ran a total of 128 miles while in the MTC. I found that exercise was much more effective in keeping my energy levels up than was taking a nap. Also, while the average elder in my district gained about ten pounds during their two months in Provo, I lost ten pounds, which was a result of not stuffing myself at every meal and utilizing a constant exercise routine. I am not inferring that every missionary should set the goal to lose weight (I just happened to have a few extra pounds to lose); Neither am I advocating exercise in every free minute. But a missionary will learn better and have much more energy if he chooses to exercise often, eat healthy, and take few naps. Personally, I feel that a nap on Sunday can be a great booster, but during the remainder of the week it is not necessary to take naps, due to the time allotted for sleep at night. Also, naps can be very habit forming, which can be quite a damper on one's alertness and energy levels.

These counselings might seem to be petty recommendations, but I have a very strong testimony of the effect that exercise has on the body. So many times, when I felt tired in the MTC, I would run a few miles and my lack of energy would turn into an excess of energy. I was so fired up and excited to learn a language and teach the gospel that I just hated to sleep. There were even a couple of times when I laid down in my bed to take a nap and then would not be able to sleep because I realized that the Lord would give me the strength that I needed to accomplish all of the personal goals that I had set for myself, and therefore a short nap was not necessary. I was not about to let a little bit of fatigue impede me from reaching my potential.

Writing letters home. I am not here to tell anyone that there is no need to write letters to family and friends while in the MTC. Since I am a convert of the church and the only current member of my family, I feel that it is important that we write to our relatives often to tell them of our experiences, personal goals and changes, and accomplishments. When writing a letter to a member of the family, it is critical that the letter be positive as well as motivational. A letter that just tells of all the hardships and difficulties that a missionary is facing will uplift no one. Bear your testimony to your family and friends and do everything that you can to help your less-active friends to get back on track. You will be amazed at the difference that you will make if you are diligent in writing letters to your friends and family that are in need of a helping hand. Also, it is important for you to know that you will probably not have time to write all of the letters you want to write on your P-day, and you should therefore accept the fact, just as I did many times, that it is likely that you just won't have time to write to everyone that you would like.

Testimony. I cannot fully explain in words just how important the MTC was in setting the tone for my mission as well as my life. When I say that the MTC is comparable to Heaven on earth, I really mean it. I love that wonderful place! Knowing how strongly I felt the Spirit makes me yearn for the day when I can live in such a celestial paradise again. I can honestly say that, more than any other time in my life, I used every spare second to prepare myself for the mission field. I have no doubt that if a missionary sets high goals and does all that is in his power to reach these goals, Heavenly Father will always provide the means to accomplish the task. I greatly desire that all missionaries make the most of their MTC experiences through patience, love, humility, and hard work. I know that if a missionary exercises these qualities he will leave the MTC with a burning desire to reap the harvest of souls that the Lord has prepared for him. Every trial and tribulation that I faced in the mission field was greatly lessened because of the strength that I was able to receive from the MTC. The experiences and feelings that I had during those two months are still the foundation of my testimony of this church till this day. I pray that you will taste such joy during your MTC stay. You can do it. The time to test yourself and prove your greatness is now. It is your race to win.

Chapter Three:

The First Two Months

My first few months in the mission field were quite a difficult experience. Despite my diligent preparations in the MTC, I had trouble adjusting to the schedule, people, language, physical and mental strains, etc. To be quite honest, when coming out of the MTC, I thought that nothing could slow me down. I imagined myself working my trainer into the ground and at the same time immediately catching on to the language. I was booming with confidence and desire. I would not say that I was prideful, but I would say that I underestimated the rigors that the mission field would provide.

This chapter is meant to prepare you for the first months of your mission, mainly the first two. I sincerely believe that you can receive much strength from the counsel of this chapter. Almost every recommendation that I give in this chapter is based on my own reflections of my training experience, as well as the experiences that I had with the five missionaries that I trained later on in my mission. My first few months in the mission field would have been much easier if I had just followed the admonishments of this chapter. I will also talk about some of the things that I did in my training, which helped me to develop my missionary skills and become more engulfed in bringing people unto Christ. Being a "greenie" does not have to be difficult, especially if a missionary knows what to expect and how to deal with the obstacles that he comes in contact with. Hopefully this chapter will give you a good idea of what these obstacles are and how you can overcome them when those times come.

The plane ride. You have finally taken off from the MTC. Your flight to your mission will most likely be an early one and you still may be tired because of your lack of sleep the night before after packing and saying your many good-byes. Hopefully you were not up too late, because if you slept very little, chances are that you will soon be paying for it. Every feeling in the world is probably running through your head right now, including nervousness, excitement, enthusiasm, and humility. The flight to your designated area could be a very long one, and so it is necessary that you do all that is possible to rest and then begin to realize your calling by talking to everyone you can with regards to the Plan of Salvation.

My trip to Chile took over twenty four hours, which gave me much time to talk to a variety of people along the way. As I headed from the Salt Lake Airport to Denver on a forty-five-minute flight, I was seated next to a girl who was in her early twenties. The look on her face told me that she was not too excited to be sitting next to me and that she obviously had a lot on her mind. At first, I was rather afraid to attempt to have a conversation with her. As I sat in my seat for a few minutes I realized that I could either open my mouth or I could waste a perfect opportunity that the Lord had given me to talk to someone about the gospel. Finally, I introduced myself to the young lady. She hesitantly told me her name and quickly looked away as if to give me the hint to stop the conversation. I was undeterred in my efforts and then proceeded to tell her that I was a missionary for the The Church of Jesus Christ of Latter-day Saints and that I was on my way to Chile. She then responded in a somewhat harsh manner by telling me that she knew all about Mormonism and what my calling was all about. At this point in the conversation I was a little unsure of what to say. I was not used to being rejected, especially since I had never really talked much about the gospel to my friends and family. Notwithstanding these feeling, I took a deep breath and began to talk again, but this time I focused on what I was feeling with respect to leaving my family and friends for two years. I told this young lady that I was nervous and afraid because my Spanish was so terrible and I still was so young in the church. I told her how I was baptized when I was seventeen and that I was the only member of the Church in my family. After I had talked for a few minutes, I noticed that the countenance of this person changed quite a bit. She appeared and acted more relaxed. I was actually building a relationship of trust!

I then told her that I was not there to preach to her, mainly because I could tell that other members of the church had preached her to many times before. As soon as she felt this comfort zone around me, she began to completely open herself up to me and tell me about her life. I quickly learned that she was also a member of the church and that she had been inactive for a long time. Her mother had also been a member at one time, but had been excommunicated. She had gone through a difficult life of drugs, sadness, and poor direction. As I heard this young women tell me her life story, I began to feel much compassion for her. Once she had told me about all she had dealt with in her life, she then started to ask me questions regarding Church doctrine. I quickly found out that she was not in agreement with the law of tithing; she believed that the church was wrong in its view of homosexuality, and she also thought that the church was prejudiced because of the fact that African-Americans did not receive the priesthood until the late twentieth century. To tell you the truth, I was somewhat baffled by all of her doubts and I realized that by trying to explain the reasons for our church's doctrine to someone that had so many negative feelings toward the church was very ineffective.

After attempting to resolve her concerns I then decided the best thing that I could do was share with her my testimony that I knew that the Book of Mormon was true, and that I could therefore not deny the revelations of the churches leaders. After I had finished sharing my testimony with her, the plane landed in Denver and we had to part our ways. We said our good-byes and as I shook her hand to wish her luck, she wished me luck also, as her faced beamed with a smile. I could tell that she had probably felt the Spirit in that airplane for the first time in a long time. I was elated that I had opened my mouth and conquered one of a missionary's biggest obstacles, which is *fear of failure.*

From this experience in the airplane I learned quite a few lessons. I learned that the Lord will put people in our paths if we are willing to share the gospel with them. I became aware of the desire that I had for inactive members to return to the Church and feel the Spirit again in their lives. I was also put in a situation where I had to exercise my skills of resolving concerns that were taught to me in the MTC. The three doubts with which I was confronted: tithing, homosexuality in the Church, and blacks and the priesthood, were all doubts that I rarely, if ever, faced while I was in Chile, mostly due to their traditional beliefs. Such an experience helped me to greatly appreciate the missionaries who stay stateside.

From Denver, my fellow group members and I headed to Miami. This flight was much longer, and we all had time to talk to the people with whom we were seated. It was such a great experience for me to see all of the missionaries in our group attempting to talk to the other passengers on the plane. Everyone had a burning desire to preach and teach that was carried over from the MTC.

On this particular flight, I was seated with another sister

missionary from my district who was also a convert. We were both excited to be finally going out to serve and we were determined to share the gospel with everyone possible. We noticed that a couple, who were probably in their fifties, were seated in front of us. We proceeded to talk with them and tell them why we were on this particular flight and our enthusiasm for what awaited us in the coming two years. After finding out about this couple and their lives, we started talking about the Church and finding out what their beliefs were with respect to religion. We soon learned that they were staunch atheists and that they had absolutely no belief in life after death. If fact, they were not even interested in the fact that we have the possibility to have eternal families after this life.

I tried my best to share my testimony with this couple, but felt that it was in vain, and that their hearts were just not yet ready to hear the gospel of Jesus Christ. The sister missionary continued to talk while I just sat down in my seat wondering how in the world anyone could not desire life, as well as paradise, after death. I was quite baffled. Eventually the sister missionary who was with me ended the conversation after she realized that this couple was not going to budge no matter what she said.

Although we did not have much success with this particular contact, we did learn many lessons from the experience. Just as I had learned in the previous flight, missionaries who serve in the states have many difficult barriers to cross in order to preach the gospel. During my two years in Chile, I met one atheist. The rest were either Catholic or Protestant. I respect a missionary so much who deals with and converts non-Christians on a daily basis. Because of this experience, I learned that sometimes it does not matter how much a missionary does or says; some people are just not yet ready to accept the gospel. In such cases, all we can do is attempt to plant a seed. We will talk about this more in depth later on in the book, but for now I will say that being able to distinguish between people who are prepared to hear the gospel and people who are not is an important aspect in being the most effective missionary that one can be.

The final segment of the flight to my mission headquarters in Osorno, Chile was from Miami to Santiago and then to Puerto Montt, a city located near Osorno. I did not have the opportunity to talk with anyone on this flight due to our seating locations, but I did notice that one of the missionaries in my group stayed up most of the night sharing the gospel with a Hispanic man in his mid-thirties. I was amazed at the missionary's bravery in attempting to talk Spanish with this gentleman, and also at the success that he was having. The elder taught the man the whole first discussion and even got his address so that he could send the missionaries to his house. Upon hearing all that this "greenie" had done despite his imperfections in the language, I realized that the most important aspect of teaching is the desire and spirit of the teacher, and not the ability to speak perfectly in another's native tongue.

I hope that you can see that in a matter of twenty four hours, I was able to learn a variety of lessons with respect to sharing the gospel. If my group and I had not had enthusiasm during our long flight, we would certainly not have had the success that we did. Only through talking with all of the people that I had been seated with was I able to learn so much and actually feel like a missionary. As missionaries, we must be constantly analyzing the actions that we take as well as the actions of others, which is what I did in the conversations that I had with these people. A mission can be a wonderful learning experience, but this will only occur if we are always analyzing our surroundings and ourselves.

Strive to be an enthusiastic and aggressive missionary from the start and see that you waste no time in sharing the gospel once you have left the MTC. Your flight, no matter how long or how short, will be filled with opportunities for you change the lives of your brothers and sisters who have yet to see the blessings of The Plan of Salvation. You will also have the opportunity to develop your skills as a representative of Jesus Christ. I know this to be true because it happened to me as well as all of the missionaries in my travel group, and it can also happen to you.

Meeting your mission president. Finally, the plane has landed and you can now see what your home will look like for the next two years. Fatigue, nervousness, excitement, as well as mental and physical exhaustion could be just a few of the feelings that you are having at this moment. For many missionaries, these first few days can be quite a grueling experience because of the lack of sleep that occurs in the final days of the MTC as well as during the flight to the mission field. Upon getting off the plane, your mission president and the assistants will likely be there to welcome you. After some handshakes and a few slaps on the back, you will be headed to the mission home. Despite the fatigue that you likely have at this moment, it is necessary to be alert, enthusiastic, and energetic while in the mission home. There, your mission president will give you many instructions and you will also be informed where your first area of service will be. It is possible that your mission president will interview you to get to know you a little better and also to receive guidance as to whom you would be best suited with in your first proselyting area. Again, I would exhort all missionaries to do the best that they possibly can during this time period to soak in the counsel of the mission president because his words can be quite an anchor of faith for you at the beginning of, as well as throughout, your mission.

Be yourself while in the mission home. Do not try to put on a show for the president, or anyone else for that matter. Some missionaries tend to be a little conceited or prideful at first because they want everyone to be impressed by their knowledge and abilities. Usually the opposite occurs and everyone else gets a bad first impression of the elder. Relax, learn, and uplift the rest of the missionaries that are with you in your travel group and in the mission home.

I remember well my first day in Chile. As I flew over that great country I admired the scenery and contemplated the next two years of my life. Despite my need for sleep on the plane, it was difficult to do so because of the excitement and adrenaline that I was experiencing. When I got off the plane, I immediately noticed the mission president and another surge of energy came over me as I saw the spiritual general who would guide me for the next two years of my life. I felt a reverence for him that matched no previous description. When we got to the mission home, we all sat down and he began to lecture us. Shortly thereafter, he realized that we did not have our notebooks out. We were then lightly chastised and admonished to write down his counsel. At that moment I realized the importance of keeping records while out in the mission field, and the reader can be rest assured that for the rest of my mission, whenever the president, his wife, or the assistants talked, I took diligent notes on the information that they gave me.

Meeting your trainer. I remember well what it was like the first time that I met my trainer in the mission field. I had taken a four-hour bus ride to the small town that would be my first area. As the bus pulled in, I noticed my companion before I saw anyone else. He stood out from the rest of the Chilean people because of his blond hair and white shirt and tie. For me, it was such a relief to see him, since I had no means of communication and I was quite afraid of everything that I was about to go through. His name was Elder Haven and was from California. He took me back to our "pension"(the house where we would be staying), and told me to unpack my things as quickly as possible. He also told me that I could take a short nap if I wanted to, but we would be leaving the pension at 6:00. I realized that it was already after 4:00 and so I had less than two hours to do all that I needed to do. I was in serious need of sleep and, to be quite honest, the only thing that I wanted to do upon my arrival was crash in my bed for a few hours. My enthusiasm had been spent. Finally, the previous days had taken their toll.

I figured that my companion would let me get all unpacked before we left to proselyte, but such was not the case. Much to my dismay, we were out the door of the pension at 6:00 precisely. I had not yet finished my packing nor had I a wink of sleep. In the eyes of Elder Haven, these tasks that I had yet to complete were non-pertinent things and would just have to wait. Although I did not fully understand, I went along with my companion without complaining and before I knew it, we were on the streets of a little town in southern Chile, preaching the restored gospel of Jesus Christ. I was also quick to realize that my companion was a fast walker. In Chile, the missionaries don't have bikes or cars, and the only means of transportation is walking. When I got to the mission field, I was in great shape physically; when my mission president told me that my companion was a fast walker, I figured that he would be no match for me considering the excellent physical shape that I was in. Well, that first night of proselyting taught me to never underestimate how fast a man can walk. I literally had to run alongside Elder Haven. His legs were no longer than mine but he still seemed to have a stride that made me look like I was crawling. I am grateful for the lesson that my companion taught me on the first day of my mission.

He taught me that the time we have in the mission field is a gift from God and there is not a minute to lose. If the White Handbook says that a missionary is to leave his apartment at 6:00, then that is when the companionship should be out the door, and, once out of the door, they should walk with vigor and enthusiasm. Elder Haven could have easily left after 6:00 the day of my arrival, but he was not about to let any blessings from Heavenly Father slip through his fingers, and he was also set on giving his "son" the correct example of an obedient missionary.

Yes, my trainer one of the hardest-working missionaries in the mission. Before my arrival in Chile, I had promised myself that I would be a diligent worker so that at the end of my service, I would not have any regrets with respect to the efforts that I had put forth. When I met my trainer, I told him that I was willing to work and that I did not want him to hold back his efforts just because of my lack of time in the mission field. After the first couple of days in the mission field, though, I was regretting this statement because I felt absolutely exhausted and overwhelmed. I struggled to handle all of the pressures that had been given me and I was feeling quite lost. I remember quite well feeling like I was following my companion around, running to keep up with him and doing my best not to get frustrated. I did not feel like I was doing very much to help our companionship and I quite often wondered if Elder Haven understood the difficulties that I was having. After the first couple of days in the field, I wrote this in my journal:

"...We are busy tending to the members. I'm basically worthless to him (my companion) right now. I can't speak, I can't plan, and I'm not full of ideas. To say that I am frustrated would be a mild understatement..."

As you can see, I was frustrated and my faith in my abilities was wavering. I think many missionaries feel some, if not all, of the feelings that I dealt with during the first weeks of my mission. As missionaries, we must accept the fact that we are not perfect and that we need the help of others, especially our companion and Heavenly Father.

After the first couple of days of my training had gone by, I finally got the chance to rest a little on P-day. Elder Haven and I had a little more time to talk about how things were going for me. I told him that I was feeling frustrated and that I didn't feel that he was too interested in all of the problems that I was dealing with. He then informed me that such was not the case, it was just that he, too, had many worries, which included being branch president, district leader, and finding new people to teach. As he explained to me all of the things that he had to worry about on a daily basis, I was baffled by how he could accomplish so much with such little help. How could I have been so selfish? I had only been thinking about me and my problems.

At this point I realized that I was the one that needed to be a little more understanding and therefore needed to put myself in the shoes of my trainer. Instead of feeling sorry for myself and being frustrated because of my trainer, I needed to start focusing more on being the best missionary that I could be. I needed to pull my weight more in our companionship. From that day on, I began to work harder and before long my attitude had improved drastically.

Receiving the call of trainer is quite a responsibility, especially in foreign speaking missions where the new missionaries cannot speak the language, which causes the trainer to have to do the majority of the teaching, planning, and worrying, unless the new missionary is exceptionally prepared, which is a very uncommon occurrence. This is why it is so critical that all new missionaries pull their weight when they enter into the mission field. If a "greenie" attempts to engulf himself with thoughts of how to reach and teach more people, as well as how he can help his trainer more effectively, he will then catch the vision more quickly of how to be a successful missionary. Otherwise, he will be caught up in unimportant obstacles that are discouraging as well as detrimental.

Pulling your weight. I have just talked about the importance of pulling your weight as a new missionary. One very important way in which a missionary can do this is through the planning sessions that take place everyday in the companionship. As you arrive at each new area in your mission, you will see that it is difficult to participate much in the daily planning because of your lack of knowledge of the area, members, and investigators. After the first week in a new area, the missionary should be relatively familiar with such components and should then be very participatory in the planning sessions. One of the things that I could have done better as a greenie was to learn the geography in my first area faster. I did not pay enough attention to the street signs, nor did I do my best to try to remember where each member lived. Because of this, it took me a few weeks until I felt comfortable knowing where I was going. It is a must that planning sessions have the full participation of both missionaries. If one missionary is not participating, he will not be able to leave his apartment with a focus of knowing what he is to do and how he is going to accomplish the goals that have been set. If you ever find yourself in a position where your companion tends to try and do the planning by himself, let him know that you are very interested in helping him and that you desire to be a part of the decision-making process in the companionship. Each missionary in a companionship is entitled to the same amount of inspiration, no matter how much time a person has had in an area. Do not think that because you are just beginning your mission that you cannot take an active part in the planning sessions each day. More often than not, your companion desires your help as well as the new ideas that you will bring to the companionship.

When you are a new missionary and you have your first companion, it will be important that you two get to know each other a little bit. Take the time to talk to your companion and show interest in his family, home, and hobbies. When a bond develops between two missionaries, they will become more effective teachers of men because of the love and spirit that will radiate. You will be amazed at just how well members and investigators can tell if a companionship does not get along. This is why you must promise yourself, just as you did in the MTC, that you will always find a way to make things work well with your companion.

He's the trainer, you're the trainee. Before I left on my mission, one of my friends gave me some very good advice. He told me to do my best to make my trainer companion feel like the *senior* companion. At the time when he told me this, I did not fully understand his counsel but when I arrived in the mission field, I attempted to allow my trainer to feel like he was basically in charge of the companionship. Oftentimes, new missionaries try to "run the show" when they first get out in the mission field, which causes a friction in the companionship. When a mission president has to decide on transfers every six weeks, the first thing that he will often do with his two assistants is choose who the trainers will be for the new missionaries. This is done even before the zone and district leaders are chosen, mainly because the calling of "trainer" is by far one of the most important callings in the mission. Remember this if you ever find yourself in disagreement with your trainer. You may feel that your idea or solution is the proper way of going about a certain task, but your companion, due to his experience, has been in that position more than once before, and therefore knows the best method of accomplishing the task or resolving the problem.

I can remember many times when I would silently question why my trainer would do certain things. Sometimes I even questioned my trainer directly why he did some of the things that he did, but usually after some time I would realize that he had made the right decision and that I just needed to have faith in his methods, all the while giving him input on what I felt we could do to have more success. Many times, when I would recommend something to my trainer, he would take my advice and we would benefit. Other times, when I would give him recommendations, he would hear me out, but not follow the ideas that I had given. When this occurred, I would just remind myself that he had the authority to make such decisions and I would be sure to find out eventually why he had not decided to follow my ideas. The funny thing was that I usually did eventually realize why he did not agree with me and I would be thankful that he had not taken my suggestion.

In the last chapter I talked about getting along with your companion and what we must do to get the most out of each companionship. The same principles apply with new missionaries and their trainers. It is critical that we commit to ourselves that we are going to find a way to get along with our trainer and all of companions thereafter. We must be humble, and understanding of the fact that we are not perfect and our companion, no matter how great or poor a missionary we think he is, can help us improve on the weaknesses that we have.

Make sure that your trainer feels important and that he knows that you respect the authority that he holds. Love him and appreciate him. He will have quite a profound influence on your mission, and possibly your life. I also hope that if you ever have any companion who makes decisions that are against mission rules that you will talk to him about the problems that he is having as well as to the mission president if such is needed. Disobedience is not to be taken lightly.

Dare to be humble. During the first few weeks of my mission, as I stated earlier, I was having quite a bit of difficulty with the language. It was very hard for me to teach the discussions because I was so nervous and afraid of messing up that I did not speak loudly enough. This caused the investigators to not fully understand what was being taught and I often had to repeat myself or my companion would just have to jump in and help me out.

One day, after we had just finished teaching a discussion, my companion addressed the problem that I was having with my volume. He simply told me that I was doing a good job but I just needed to try and speak up a little louder. As soon as he said this I snapped back and said that I was doing my best and that there was no reason why the investigators should have a problem hearing me. Elder Haven, being the wise and experienced trainer that he was, told me to just think about it and he said that he would not say any more about it. If my memory serves me well, I think I just grumbled a little bit and felt sorry for myself the rest of the day. That night and the proceeding morning, I thought a lot about what he had told me and I realized that he was absolutely right, and that I needed to focus on speaking louder and on voice projection during the discussions. I also came to the conclusion that I was acting immaturely for not wanting to accept his advice and that I needed to repent and improve my attitude. This I quickly did and immediately I could see a difference in the way I taught the discussions. In fact, people stopped asking me to repeat myself after each principle that I taught and the discussions that my trainer and I taught were therefore a more spiritual experience for everyone.

Upon reflecting on the person that I was when I entered into the mission field, I realize that in many ways I was not a very humble person, and many times my pride would keep me from overcoming my weaknesses. The good thing is, though, that I eventually was able to improve these aspects of my personality and therefore fully learn from my fellow missionaries. In my first two months, I was lucky enough to be trained by two of the greatest and hardest-working missionaries that ever set foot on Chilean soil. Because of my prideful attitude and lack of understanding, I sometimes gave these two wonderful men a hard time about the way they went about things or the decisions that they made. I realize that I was immature in many ways at that early point in my mission, and as I progressed throughout those two years and was able to be a trainer myself so many times, my love and respect for my two "dads" grew tremendously. I often regretted the roller-coaster mood that I was in those first two months of my mission and I many times since have expressed to my first two companions the amazing effect that they had on my mission as well as my life. I feel a great amount of love and admiration for those two men. They changed me forever and helped mold me into the person that I am today. I know that your trainer will also have a powerful effect on your mission; especially if you do everything you can to learn from him and better yourself through his example. I also know that not every missionary is as lucky as I was because some trainers just aren't as good examples as others. Even though many times this is the case, it is possible you will learn what *not* to do from your trainer, which will in turn prepare you for the decisions that you will make later on in your mission when it is your turn.

Meeting your Goals: Missionary Certification

In the previous chapter, we talked about the importance of goals and the need to have goals as a missionary. Most missions have goals already set for new missionaries before they ever even reach the field. This was also the case in my mission, in which the goals of all missionaries for the first two months were:

—Memorize the first two discussions
—Memorize 15 scriptures (listed in discussions)
—Read all of the Book of Mormon
—Memorize Doctrine and Covenants Section 4 in Spanish

Actually, the goals that I just listed are part of a missionary certification system used in our mission as well as many other missions in the world. These certification programs are used to help all elders and sisters have a clear vision of what their studies will be throughout their missions. They may develop a sense of accomplishment upon completing each of the levels that are specified in the certification system.

These weren't the only goals that the new missionaries were to meet, but these were the main ones. As you can probably see, these were lofty goals given to us by the mission president. Many beginning missionaries questioned why they should be given so much to do in their first months, but the answer was a simple one: If a missionary does not have any clear goals as to what he should be studying or doing at all times, chances are that he is wasting much of his and the Lord's time. Also, in most missions, the president wants to help the new elders and sisters to gain work ethic, confidence, as well as the guidance of the spirit through their studies.

Attacking your goals intelligently. I have already mentioned in this chapter the fact that I stressed out quite a bit during my first two months in the mission field, and the missionary certification goals given me were part of the reason why I felt so lost at times. All missions have different schedules as to when missionaries are to wake up, how long a lunch break they have, and what time they are to be in at night. These schedules vary for a variety of reasons, but mainly because of the diverse cultures of the many countries in which the Church is located. In my mission, we were given about two hours in the morning as well as two hours in the afternoon to study. Although this might seem like a lot of time, it always amazed me as to how fast the hours would fly by when I was studying. Since I was given so many goals to pass to reach the first level of missionary certification, I was always spending a certain amount of time each day working on them. For example, I would spend thirty minutes studying my scriptures, then thirty on my discussions, then ten minutes on D&C section 4, etc. Initially, I would get really frustrated because it was taking me so long to memorize everything and I seemed to not be retaining the information very well. After a few weeks I realized that I was spending too much time studying *everything* and not enough time studying just one thing. Therefore, I started to focus more on my discussions and I didn't worry much about the scriptures that I was supposed to memorize. Instead of reading each scripture fifty times a day, I read each one just once a day for about thirty days. This consumed very little time but what it did do was help me memorize the fifteen scriptures as well as Doctrine and Covenants 4 without even realizing it or putting much effort into it. After I had read the scriptures everyday for that month or so, I finally attempted to memorize the selected scriptures completely, and it took about two days to memorize them all! I was ecstatic that the method had worked. In fact, at the end of my first two months of training, I had completed the first level of certification and had the first four discussions memorized. I followed this same technique with the five missionaries that I trained and each time they were successful in achieving their certification goals on time.

I hope that you can see that the best way to accomplish goals on your mission, when it comes to memorizing certain scriptures or discussions, is by attacking the goals individually. This method will help you to not waste your time by trying to accomplish too much at once and overloading your brain, which leads to stress and frustration. I've been there and felt overwhelmed by the many tasks confronting me, but I learned from my mistakes and I eventually was able to maximize my missionary study time.

Memorizing: all day, everyday. I have a few other tips that I would like to share with you with respect to memorizing. About ninety nine percent of all missionaries do not have a photographic memory and cannot memorize the discussions in a few days. The excuse "I can't memorize the discussions because my memory is so terrible," is just that—an excuse. Don't be one of those missionaries who accepts the notion that he has a "bad" memory and therefore cannot memorize the discussions. Memorization is a difficult task for everyone. Success is based purely on the effort that one elects to put out.

I never went anywhere during my first two months in the mission field without my printed discussions. I had them folded in such a way that they could fit right in my shirt pocket and I could study them whenever I had a little bit of free time. Whenever I was riding in a bus or walking down a street, I was normally studying my discussions. I studied so much everyday that my head always seemed to be hurting a little bit because of all the reading that I did. I couldn't stand wasting any time. Just as in the MTC, I basically ate, drank, and slept the discussions. I loathed having to read them in real discussions with investigators so much that I just decided to push myself as hard as possible and memorize them quickly. This is why it only took me two and a half months to memorize all six, which is quite a feat considering that it normally takes about six months for missionaries to memorize their discussions in another language. We can pray for help (as we should) to memorize the discussions, but if we don't put out 110% on our own part, the Lord has no reason to bless us to accomplish such a task. This is not to say that prayer isn't an important aspect in helping us to more quickly memorize our discussions or other scriptures. Actually, prayer and hard work go hand-in-hand, and must be accompanied by each other throughout your mission as well as your life.

Sometimes missionaries ask why it is so important to memorize the discussions. When one repeats exactly what the discussions say, it sounds "robotic" to the investigator. I will agree with this statement in the sense that there are missionaries who do sound like robots as they are reciting the discussions, but this only occurs because the missionary has memorized the discussion poorly and has not practiced enough in trying to make his presentations sound more natural and fluid. It is very important that you learn the discussions so well that you can say them naturally. I taught most of my discussions word for word, along with adding my own tid-bits here and there. Once I had learned the discussions well, I was never accused of sounding robotic because I had diligently practiced saying them so that the investigator felt as if we really were having a "discussion."

It's called a discussion for a reason. My trainer spent quite a bit of time practicing his discussions. Whenever we had an appointment to teach an upper-level discussion, I would see him practicing his presentation beforehand while we were still in our apartment. When we would arrive at the houses of the investigators to teach the discussion, he would never open up his discussion booklets, whether it was the first discussion or the sixth. At first, upon seeing this, I was amazed that he could teach an entire lesson without looking to see where he was in the discussion booklet. Even more amazing was just how relaxed he looked whenever he taught a discussion. If I had not known that he was reciting the discussion word for word, I would have thought that he was just carrying on a conversation about the gospel. This example taught me a lot about the kind of teacher that I eventually wanted to be. It also showed me that we, as missionaries, are sent out to teach "discussions" with our investigators. Note the word "discussion" and not "lecture." A problem that many missionaries have is that they teach lectures and not discussions. This is common with new missionaries. When we are unfamiliar with the discussions, we tend to focus so much on what we are teaching and where we are in the discussion that we do not pay enough attention to what the investigator is telling us or how they feel with respect to what we are teaching. This is why it is important that we do more than just memorize the discussions. Although I did memorize the all six discussions in two and a half months, after I had completed this task I realized that I was a very long way from teaching the discussions at a level in which I felt completely comfortable and able to answer any questions that an investigator could have, without worrying about where I was in the discussion. Because of this, I practiced the discussions with my companions often so that I could immediately pick up my place in any principle of the discussions after having resolved a doubt or answered a question. Since I was able to worry over less and less over time as to where I was in the discussion, I was able to become a better listener. So often, when we ask a "find out" question as a missionary, we really don't even listen to the answer of the investigator because we are so caught up on what comes next in the discussion.

You will find this to be very true in your mission, mainly because it is a habit of most missionaries, especially when they are just beginning. You will be able to break this habit quickly if you study the discussions in such a way that you learn to pick up each part of the principles quickly and fluidly. Also, when I studied the discussions more, I became more familiar with the scriptures used in each principle of the discussions. With a stronger understanding of the scriptures, I could better explain their history and their relation to the principle of the gospel.

Voice Flexion. From my trainer and other companions, I was also able to learn the importance of voice flexion in the discussions. Missionaries often hold the same level of volume throughout the discussions, which causes the investigators to get bored or even fall asleep. I'm sure that you have been there before, finding yourself in a very boring class or sacrament meeting where the speaker doesn't change the level or energy of their voice the whole time. When a missionary constantly changes his voice from high to low in the discussions, his investigators will almost always be in tune with the lesson and therefore the Spirit will be able to thrive more strongly.

The Missionary Guide talks about how we must develop this technique as we go throughout our missions. Voice flexion is not something that we can develop in a day. It takes effort and willingness from the missionary to experiment in each discussion that he teaches so that he can learn when and where one should change his voice in order to make the discussion more stimulating to the investigator. Remember, you must be an exciting missionary to be around, whether it be in church or in an investigator's house. Voice flexion adds life to the words and teachings that are being relayed to the learner.

Developing your discussions. I have just explained the importance of "knowing" the discussions in order to be a more effective preacher and teacher of the gospel. I know that all missionaries can develop their talents so that their discussions are exciting as well as invigorating for their investigators. Practice your discussions throughout your time as a missionary. Attempt to make yourself a better teacher everyday through experimentation and hard work. If you do these things you will become a master teacher and you will also improve upon your discussions throughout your mission.

Chapter Four:

Learning a New Language

This chapter will not apply to all missionaries, but the counsel written here can be of benefit to everyone.

I feel grateful to the Lord for having had the opportunity to learn a foreign language as a missionary. Spanish is such a big part of my life and I would never have developed such a love for the language if it were not for my mission. Any missionary who is upset or worried because he has been called to speak a second language needs to understand that he has been blessed beyond his own imagination for having received such an opportunity. I hope that everyone appreciates and takes advantage of such a wonderful blessing.

The "two month" myth. In chapter two, I mentioned the fact that for me, picking up a new language was quite a difficult task. While I was in the MTC, everyone seemed to believe that a missionary who is called to a foreign language mission usually understands most of what is said to him by the natives after about two month's practice in the mission field. I have come to the conclusion that most missionaries need more than two months in order to understand all of what the natives are saying, unless one is native or has already had many high school and college courses in that new language.

Despite my diligent studies in the MTC, when I arrived to my first area in Chile I realized just how far I was from grasping the Spanish language. I vividly remember my first meal in a members' house. As I sat and ate the funny-looking pasta that they had given me, two older ladies and a young boy spoke to me. They attempted to find out more about me but I was so lost as to what they were saying that I could not answer them in the slightest bit. I was embarrassed and, to be honest, I remember wishing that they would stop asking me questions and just leave me alone.

Eventually, I finished eating and then asked my companion what they were saying and why they had been laughing. He told me that the "mamita"(the lady we lived with) was laughing because I could not understand anything. In fact, during my two month stay in my first area, all I basically did was listen to the "mamita" tell me just how slow (in grasping the language) I was, compared to the rest of the new missionaries that had started in that area. That is the wonderful thing about Latinos—the fact that they aren't afraid to be honest with you. At times I would get extremely frustrated and greatly perplexed, mainly because I could not understand why it was so difficult for me to understand even the simplest of phrases. To make matters worse, I did not know how to laugh at myself, which led to even more stress and frustration.

After I left my first area, I was placed with my first Latin companion, which helped me to speak and understand the language more clearly, but it also lead to more disappointment because I had such a hard time understanding my companion. Because of my slow learning, I eventually came to the conclusion that I was destined to never understand the Chilean people very clearly. Some of my most heartfelt prayers in my mission were during the initial months, asking for help in understanding the language better. By the time I had about five months in the mission field, things had started to get a little better, but I did not really recognize my progress because there was still much room for improvement. At one point, I contemplated going to an ear doctor to check and see if I had a hearing problem, which would therefore be the cause of my understanding difficulties. I never did go, but just thinking back on my frustrations makes me realize that I went through that time period for a good reason. Ether 12:27 reads:

> "And if man come unto me I will show unto them their weakness. I give unto men weakness that they may be humble; and my grace is sufficient for all men that humble themselves before me, for if they humble themselves before me, then will I make weak things become strong unto them."

What a true scripture! I must have read that scripture a thousand times during the first six months of my mission. To fill you in on how my struggles ended: After six months in the mission field, I was called to train a new missionary. He was just like I was at the beginning of my mission. It was difficult for him to understand and speak the language. While helping my companion to progress with his Spanish, I realized just how far I had come with my own abilities to speak to and understand the Chilean people. I also stopped worrying about my own shortcomings and instead focused my efforts in helping my companion communicate better. By doing these things, I realized that, for me, the storm had passed, and I had overcome a great trial in my life.

Bettering your communication skills. Through my own experiences as a new missionary and upon training five new missionaries, I was able to develop an understanding of the methods in which new missionaries can learn a foreign language and how they can improve their speaking techniques throughout their time in the mission field. I have listed some suggestions:

The Spanish Infield (or any other in-field book given to foreign language missionaries in the MTC). If there was one thing that drove me really nuts on my mission was hearing missionaries say that they could not learn anything by using their infield book. What a bunch of bologna! I loved my infield book. It helped me tremendously in my mission. Not only did it help me with my basic Spanish skills, but it also helped me to fine-tune and retain these skills. As a junior companion, I read the infield book two times straight through, and as a trainer, I read it again another five times. That comes to about seven times of reading that wonderful book. Although I pretty much had every page memorized by the seventh time, I seemed to learn something new every time I read it, or I at least realized that I was not using a certain rule correctly in my grammar. It was always obvious to me when an elder or sister missionary had not studied from their Spanish infield book because their basic grammar skills would often be very poor. Although a missionary can develop the ability to understand and communicate with the people in his area without studying the infield book, it is likely that he won't have a fine-tuned ability to speak the language, which will lead to a lack of understanding and also a lack of the Spirit as he teaches the people in his designated area.

Not all missionaries have the ability to sound like a native, even after spending two years in the mission field. I worked constantly on my accent while out in the mission field, and I was never able to develop a clean accent that did not immediately show that I was a "gringo." Even though I never did obtain such an accent, I was able to greatly improve on my basic pronunciation of the language. For this reason, it is rather difficult for some missionaries to sound like a native, if not impossible, but I do know, that through study of the *Spanish Infield* and other books, all missionaries can generate a very dominant use of the grammar of the language. It just takes a constant effort.

One might say that it is not important to master the rules of a foreign language to teach it successfully, but I would beg to differ. Although grammar is not everything, it is still important. When I had about six months in the field, I once went to a zone conference in which the assistants to the president were to give a few lectures on missionary work to a number of zones. One of the assistants who was just about to go home, misused his Spanish grammar so badly during a class that the missionaries listening, including myself, could only shake their heads. Instead of focusing in on the lesson of the class, I was so distracted by the onslaught of grammatical errors that I could only wonder why this missionary had not done more to develop his speaking abilities. I was not trying to judge this missionary. He was a hard worker, but the fact remains that he did not get the desired response from his audience that day because he had not enlarged his language skills. This same thing can often occur when a missionary is teaching a discussion in a second language. If one is distracting to the investigator because of his word usage, the Spirit may not be as strong.

Use your companion: a common myth among many missionaries is the idea that the more native companions that one has, the better they will speak the native language. I knew many English-speaking missionaries that had mostly native (Chilean) companions in their missions but spoke the language poorly. I also knew many missionaries that had mostly English-peaking companions who spoke Spanish well. Why does this happen? The answer is simple: many missionaries, when they have a native companion, are not humble enough to ask their companions to help them. I always told my Latin companions and friends that they had to correct me if I was mistaken. I made them promise to do this because I would just continue to make the same mistake. For some crazy reason, many English-speaking missionaries do not like it when their native speaking companions correct them or help them with the language. This lack of humility leads to bad habits which can be very difficult to break.

Don't be afraid to ask your companion to help you. Whether he speaks the native language or not, he can help you improve your speaking abilities. My first "son" in the mission, despite his initial inability to talk fluidly in Spanish, helped me to better my pronunciation. Although I had been out in the mission field much longer than he had, I still had much to improve on with regards to my pronunciation of many words. I asked him to correct me whenever I made a mistake and he willingly obliged, especially since I did not hesitate to correct him. Together, we both were able to help each other, which lead to quite a bit of learning on each of our parts. If I had not been humble enough to accept the constructive criticism of my greenie, we would never have reached our learning potential.

Keep studying throughout your mission: so many missionaries, after they have between six and eight months in the mission field, stop progressing with regards to the language. Why? I just cannot understand why anyone would want to stop learning a language when they still have so many months to go and so much to improve on. You can do many things to improve your speaking skills throughout your mission. Study the way that the natives speak. Analyze their use of the language and their patterns. Ask others about ways to improve your accent and sentence structure. Study vocabulary words by using a dictionary. Learn five new words a week. I could go on, but the main thing that you need to know is to keep learning!

I hope that you have learned from this chapter a few of the ways in which you can develop a second language to the best of your ability. Earlier in this chapter, I mentioned the effect that Ether 12:27 had on my mission. When I left to go on my mission, I "came unto the Lord," much like the scripture states. Immediately thereafter I was given a weakness (the language), which caused me to humble myself before my maker and beg for his help to overcome this obstacle. I had the faith that I would eventually improve. I studied and did my part, and eventually the Lord helped to make my Spanish become stronger.

I hope you can see, just from my experience, just how true Ether 12:27 is. It is amazing! It describes, step-by-step, exactly what I went through to obtain the ability to communicate with the Chilean people. In fact, I was so diligent with my Spanish studies throughout my mission that by the end, I was one of the better speakers in the mission. Even today, as I take Spanish courses at the college level, my instructors tell me that I have one of the best grasps that they have seen of the grammar rules of Spanish. The Lord has made a one-time weakness of mine strong! I love that! The church is so true and everything that the Book of Mormon admonishes is right on target. I challenge all missionaries who are called to learn a new language on their missions to learn to speak the best that they can. There is no limit to your abilities. All you need is a desire and a strong work ethic and with this, "all weak things will be made strong unto you!"

Chapter Five:

The Makings of a Successful Junior Companion

Congratulations! You have completed your first two months of training and you have learned more than you ever thought imaginable. In the following months, it is likely that you will be a "junior companion." I imagine that you are familiar with how the system works in the mission field. Usually, once the mission president feels that a missionary is developed enough to handle the load of a senior companion, he is then called to that position. Of course, this is not always the case. Every mission, and every mission president, has a different method of calling missionaries to certain positions.

Oftentimes, missionaries who could easily handle the responsibilities of being a senior companion are not yet called to the position. This does not mean that they are inferior missionaries in any way; it just means that the Lord has other plans for that missionary at that given moment. It is important that you always remember that a mission consists of about 190 missionaries. With such a large number of elders and sisters, it is impossible to please all missionaries with regards to their next calling, designated proselyting area, or companion. Besides, a mission president's job is not to "please" his missionaries, but rather to do the will of the Lord. This simple fact can be difficult for many to swallow.

The life of a junior companion is not always the easiest. At times, missionaries do not get along with their senior companions, which can be caused by a variety of reasons. Most of the time, problems occur because of different work ethics. If one companion is lazy and the other is very motivated, it is likely that there will be some friction. If one companion is too dominating, again friction is imminent. There are a million factors that determine the cohesion of a companionship. This is why it is so important that companions attempt to be on the same plane of thought and actions. Respect and equality can form an amazing bond between missionaries.

The purpose of this chapter is to help you to be better prepared to be a great junior companion. I also hope that this chapter helps you to enjoy, rather than abhor, the time that you spend as a junior companion in your mission.

Accept the Lord's decisions! So often, missionaries question why they have been put with another missionary. It is possible that you will one day find yourself with a companion with whom you do not completely see eye to eye. We have no control over who our companions will be while out in the mission field. Heavenly Father knows who we need to be with. We should never ask ourselves why we have been put with elder or sister so-and-so. Rather, we should seek to find out how the Lord's work can continue to go forth as we work together with our fellow companions.

At one point in my mission, I was put with an elder who was quite different than I was. Because I was young in the mission, he often was very pushy and gave little respect to the input that I had in our companionship. His patience was very short and when we were together, I was always worried that I was going to make a mistake. I could say quite a bit more here about the difficulties of our companionship, but I will not. I will just say that our actions and opinions with respect to missionary work were quite different.

This was the most trying time of my mission. For the first month with this companion, we had very little success. We did not baptize anyone and my companion had been in that area for quite some time. As I've already mentioned, we got along terribly, but I just remained patient, knowing that he was about to get transferred out of our area. By the end of our first month together, I was counting down the days when he would be transferred and I would get a new companion. I was positive that he was getting a transfer, mainly because I had informed the mission president of the problems that we were having. I was depressed and I felt like I could not take one more minute with this elder.

However, when the transfer day rolled around, we found out that we were to be together for another month. I was in shock! In fact, I was horrified! I had just had the hardest month of my life and now I had to go through another month of the same thing. I was also very confused as to why the mission president would keep us together, knowing that we were having so many problems. Eventually, I came to understand why the Lord would leave us together one more month.

As our second month got under way, we continued to have many difficulties together. I prayed constantly for help from my Heavenly Father. Every morning I would go to the bathroom alone and converse with the Lord, asking for the strength to get through that time period.

Shortly after this second month began, we started to have some success. An older lady that we had been teaching for quite some time had finally decided to be baptized. My companion had become very good friends with her, as well as her family. Not to say that I did not get along with them as well, but my companion had built a very strong relationship of trust with them over the previous months. This relationship of trust was so strong and effective that almost all of her family was baptized that second month. In a matter of four and a half weeks together, my companion and I had witnessed ten baptisms, eight being from this lovely old lady's family! It was an amazing turn of events.

But the story does not end there. One of the ladies in this family that was baptized eventually became one of the strongest members of the ward. She received her endowments at her year mark and was so active in missionary work that many of her neighbors were also baptized. In fact, just from this one woman, over thirty people had joined the church by the time I had left to go home from my mission!

Now, let's analyze the chain of events a little more clearly:

—I had an extremely difficult first month with my companion, including no baptisms.

—I hoped that there would be a transfer, but there was not.

—A wonderful old lady got baptized at the beginning of our second month together.

—Because of this lady's influence, as well as the relationship of trust that my companion had with her family, eight more members of the family were baptized during our second month.

—One of the eight became a very strong member and brought over thirty more souls into the waters of baptism over the next two years.

Can you see that the Lord's plan was quite different than mine. I had hoped that there would be a transfer, but only because I was not looking at our companionship from the perspective that maybe there was a reason for us staying together. Those difficult months taught me some very impor-tant lessons.

I learned that we should always accept our mission pres-ident's decisions. At times, we may think that we know more than he does, but this is not the case. When it comes to trans-fers, the Lord is the director, and the mission president is only acting out the Lord's will. I feel that Heavenly Father knew that my companion was a needed element in the conversion of this wonderful family. Without him, it is possible that another elder would have done things in a different way, and therefore would not have had success in getting this greatly important family to accept the church and be baptized.

I feel that my relationship with Heavenly Father grew a great amount because of this trying experience with my companion. As I said earlier, I prayed, diligently, every morning that I would be able to get along with my companion. I wanted to feel love for him. I yearned to see eye-to-eye with him, but then again, I knew that I still had to choose doing what was right over what was wrong. Through countless conversations with my Heavenly Father, my patience grew as well as my humility. Even with all the success that we ended up having, we still did not walk in unison, which was very difficult for me.

Such humility helped me to know that fighting and arguing is never excusable, nor effective, when it comes to resolving companionship problems. It is amazing just how fast arguing with one's companion can lead to the Spirit's retreat. Do not argue with your companion. It solves nothing. I know this for a fact. Only love, faith, humility, and patience can help two young missionaries overcome their differences.

Looking back on those two months, I feel that they were the most difficult two months of my life, but I also feel that I grew more in those two months than at any other point in my life. I am grateful for the trial that was given me, and I have used this experience to help me with many other trials and decisions since that time.

Throw some wood on that fire! First of all, just because you are a junior companion, this does not mean that you cannot make a huge difference in the success of your companionship. You are entitled to just as much inspiration as your fellow senior companion, the only difference between the two of you is the fact that your senior companion has the final say when it comes to making decisions. I'm sure you have heard the stories of how a junior companion has felt inspired to do something, like knocking on a certain door, and despite the doubts of the senior companion, the door was knocked and a golden family was found and baptized. Stories like this one happen all the time!

It is incredible just how much of a difference a junior companion can make if he just has a "fire" and positive attitude. It is possible that when you are out in the mission field you will be placed with a senior companion who is not very motivated to do the work. When this occurs, you have a variety of choices. You can:

—Lower your level to that of your companion, which will in turn cause you to develop poor habits and lose the spirit.

—Tell your companion that he is lazy and needs to get to work, which will in turn lead to more friction in your companionship.

—Act so excited and fired up about the area that you are in that your companion feeds off your energy and raises his level which causes you two to have an explosion of success in your area, leading to many people entering into the waters of baptism to receive the fullness of blessings in this life as well as the afterlife!

Now, you have seen your choices, which one do you plan on taking? The reason why many missionaries and senior companions are lazy is because they have never had a very positive example to give them the proper vision of what missionary work is all about. You can be that example!

Trust me when I tell you that verbally pointing out the shortcomings of your companion will almost always have a negative affect. The best way to motivate and correct your companion is to show him, by love and example the correct way of doing things. Never lower yourself to the level of your companion. I imagine that you are reading this book because you want to be the best missionary that you can be. To do this you must not settle. Do not meet your companion halfway when it comes to your enthusiasm and effort! This is not to say that compromise is not needed in a companionship to resolve some problems, because as you have read, it is very important. But such is not the case when it comes to the enthusiasm and the effort that you put out in your missionary work. Remember, you are responsible for raising the spiritual and work levels of all the missionaries that surround you. Let your enthusiasm be contagious!

Your time as a junior companion should be a great time of learning (as should the rest of your mission). During this period, you have the chance to develop yourself as a missionary. Every missionary that you will ever work with is different. No two missionaries teach or act exactly alike. As you grow, progress, and mature in the mission field, you will be able to take the best of what you have seen from others and apply that to your own attributes and teaching techniques. You will also learn what *not* to do from your companions. As you analyze their strengths and weaknesses, you will be able to get a clear vision of exactly the type of missionary that you want to be. This is why it is so important that you reflect on everything that you and others do as a missionary. Only through such reflection can you begin to reach your potential out in the mission field.

During my first six months in the mission field, I learned a tremendous amount from my senior companions. Once, I sat down and wrote a list of the main things that I had learned from each companion:

Month #1—Elder Haven: He taught me how to work harder than I had previously thought possible. He walked faster than any man that I had ever seen, therefore showing me the need to not waste a second in the mission field. He also taught me the importance of memorizing the discussions.

Month #2—Elder Balls: He taught me what the "pure love of Christ" really is. He loved people so much that they could see Christ in his eyes, which lead to amazing success in converting souls to Christ.

Month #3 and 4—Elder Orellana: He taught me the need to work through members and the great amount of success that can be wrought through them.

Month #5—Elder Rockwood: He taught me how to knock doors successfully, and just how effective door approaches can be if done with the right attitude.

Month #6—Elder Degraff: He helped me a great deal with

my Spanish, which was a critical step towards enabling me to become a trainer the following month.

As you can see, each one of the companions that I was blessed enough to have during my first six months in the mission field taught me a great deal about the type of missionary that I wanted to be. Although I did learn many good habits from these young men, I also learned and saw things that I thought could have been done differently, and so I attempted not to make the same mistakes when my time came to be a senior companion.

Planning and communication. It is tremendously important that you attempt to converse with your companion often. Let him know how you are feeling, especially about your area. Make suggestions whenever you feel prompted to do so. Hopefully, you will do this as a greenie and continue the habit while you are a junior companion. The Lord has commanded that missionaries preach the gospel in twos because he knows that that is the way they can be most successful. If one missionary makes all of the decisions while the other never gives input, a companionship will not reach its full potential. You must live your mission with the belief that you need your companion and he needs you.

Planning goes hand-in-hand with communication. As a missionary, you should be planning and thinking about your investigators and your area all the time. This planning can be done individually or as a team. Once again, the way to maximize your effectiveness is by walking in unison in all of your actions as a companionship. Do not let your companion plan without you. It will hurt the both of you. It will also hurt the chance of your investigators getting baptized. Promise yourself that such a mutual focus will be achieved in every companionship that you have.

Companionship Inventory Meeting. From day one in the MTC, you are taught to have at least one companionship inventory meeting per week. The sad thing is that many missionaries do not take this meeting seriously and therefore there is little improvement on their relationship or the success that they are having in their area. Here is an example of a classic inventory meeting:

> *Elder A:* Uhhhhm, well, how are we doing?
> *Elder B:* Good. Well, I guess that says it then, we are doing just fine!

As you can see, nothing got accomplished in this meeting between Elder A and Elder B. Because so many missionaries are afraid to address any problems with their companions, such a meeting is all too common in the MTC as well as in the mission field. A true companionship inventory meeting should have an agenda, just like any other church meeting, consisting of hymns, prayer, and testimony. It is critical that the Spirit is invited to the meeting, and that each participant expresses any concerns that he may be having at that moment. For example, if you feel that your companion does not pay enough attention to your thoughts and ideas, you should tell him, in a loving manner, what you are feeling. In another example, if you feel the need to apologize to your companion for any reason what-soever, now is a great time to do so (as well as any other time). One thing that I always did with my companions was brain-storm things that we were doing well and also things that we could improve on. When doing these brainstorming activities, we were able to set many excellent goals for the upcoming week. There are so many more things that can be done during inventory meetings. Also, I think that it is good to talk about the personal goals that each missionary has, that way companions can verify each other each week and also motivate each other at the same time.

I bear you my testimony of the importance of inventory meetings as a companionship while in the mission field. By having these meetings weekly in my mission, I was able to form much stronger relationships with my companions and I was also able to create a feeling of togetherness and consecration with these young men. Make no excuses. Set the goal to have these meetings every week, and then complete your goal. If you do this, I know that your mission will be a much better and happier experience.

To close this chapter on life as a junior companion, I just want to reiterate my thoughts on the importance of learning as much as possible from your companion during this time period. It does not matter if you are a junior companion for one month or for two years, you can still grow, progress, learn, and change many lives.

Chapter Six:

Parenthood

Congratulations! Way to go! You are going to be a father! (Sisters, you can look forward to motherhood.) Your time has come to be a trainer. Boy do I wish that I were in your position! The following months will be some of the most educational months of your life up to this date. You will be amazed at the amount of learning that will be wrought within you if you have the right mindset.

In my mission, I had the pleasure, and I really stress the word *pleasure*, to train five new missionaries. If fact, I was a trainer for eight straight months of my mission. I cherish that time of my mission. I still feel the utmost respect and love for those five wonderful men that I had the opportunity to help get started on the right foot as they began their missions in such a distant and foreign land. I wanted each one of those individuals to be the best missionary that they could possibly be. Much of their success depended on their efforts, but another critical factor in their success depended on the things that I taught them the first few months of their service to the Lord.

Needless to say, I took a great amount of pride in my five "sons." I yearned that they would be able to see the potential that they had and could also witness many faithful souls enter into the waters of baptism during their two year service. I took my responsibility of being called as a trainer very seriously. I took pride in everything that my new missionaries could do. It pains me to see missionaries, especially trainers, that don't really care about their ability to shape a young man's mission.

I was blessed enough to be trained by incredible missionaries from the beginning. I was able to see and learn what type of missionary I wanted to be. So many missionaries drift through their missions only because they have never had the opportunity to work with other great missionaries. If you, as a trainer, work to instill a vision in your greenie, his whole mission will be drastically changed. But in that same regard, if you are a slacker and you do not have the needed vision and example as a trainer, it is likely that your new missionary will follow in your footsteps. Therefore, I say to you to take the calling of trainer more serious than any other calling you have had up to this point in your life so far. You cannot comprehend just how many lives will be changed, for better or for worse, through the actions that you make as a trainer.

I have written this chapter so that you will be better prepared to train a new missionary. I will be honest with you in saying that it is not always the easiest thing to do, especially when they experience difficulties adjusting to mission life. Also, it is possible that you will not get the opportunity to train a greenie in your mission. Such is the Lord's way, but this does not mean that these principles can't be applied to any companion or fellow missionary that you work with during your time out in the field. In fact, this counsel is applicable to just about any circumstance that you may encounter during your missionary service.

First things first. Every missionary is different, unique, and special in his or her own way. It is critical that you learn as much about your companion as you can when he arrives in the mission. If you take the time to ask him questions and learn about his life, you will be benefited in a variety of ways. First of all, if you show your greenie that you are interested in him, he will likely be more willing to open up to you and also put his trust in you. He will say to himself something like, "Wow, my trainer wants to know about me, he seems like a pretty good guy." This may sound a little goofy, but think about it. How did you feel when you first arrived in your mission? (You may not be in the field yet, so ask yourself this question when the time comes.) In many missions, especially the foreign ones, greenies feel completely lost and sometimes alone in their new environments. As a trainer, you can ease the difficulty of this transition period by showing your companion sincere interest in him as a person. This interest will also help you to learn ways in which your companion can help in the success of converting other people unto the gospel. For example, if your companion is a wonderful singer, this could be an advantage in bringing the Spirit into your discussions. My trainer used the fact that I was a new convert and a former member of the Catholic faith to our advantage. This helped us relate better to the largely Catholic Chilean people and also helped me feel important to our companionship. Another example of how knowing your companion can help is the fact you will better be able to spot a problem that is occurring with your companion and therefore help him to overcome his diffi-culties. (An example is being dumped by a girlfriend right before the mission.) Enough said on this subject. Take the time to get to know your companion and the benefits will follow.

The Pep Talk. "The Pep Talk" is a very important aspect to the success of your training experience, but I do not recommend "the talk" to everyone. I used it five times and it always paved the way to the success that my greenie and I had with each other. "The Pep Talk" should take place a few hours after you meet your greenie. By this point, you should have learned quite a bit about him, that is, of course, unless he has been asleep because of his jet lag. I shall give you an example of what needs to be said in "The Pep Talk":

Trainer: Elder Smith, I am excited that you are my companion. We are going to have a great time together. I feel like I was in your shoes just yesterday. I was quite confused as to the many things that I had to deal with at the beginning of my mission, and therefore please do not hesitate to ask me any questions that you may have. You are in for the best two years of your life. I just want you to know that I am a hard worker and we are going to do all that is possible to convert people unto the Savior. I also want you to know that I care very much for your personal progress as a missionary, and so I will do many things to help you improve on the many facets of missionary work. How do you feel about that?

Elder Smith: That sound great to me. I'm just excited to work hard. Also, I'm a little nervous about learning this new language. I had a tough time grasping things while in the MTC.

Trainer: You need not worry. We will definitely work hard and I will help you to better grasp the language at a quicker rate. I want you to know that you can trust the advice that I will give you. I will not lead you astray in any aspect, but I also need to know that I can depend on you to do what is asked of you. There will be times when I ask you to do things, and you will most likely feel incapable or confused. I can understand these feelings because I often had them with my own trainer. Now, in retrospect, I realize that the things he had me do were only for my benefit. He wanted to help me to become great. I feel the same about you. I promise you that we will be obedient, hard working, and have a lot of fun doing it. I also promise that I will never ask you to do anything that I would not do myself, nor will I push you any harder than I push myself. Will you be willing to go along with that, elder?

Elder Smith: You've got my promise.

As you can see, this was a very simple conversation, but also a very monumental one. Upon having this talk, a new missionary will be much less hesitant when you ask him to do a door approach the first time. He will also be more willing to give a talk, make a contact, or practice the language with you while walking down the street. Now, of course you mustn't ever take advantage of this commitment or problems will undoubtedly arise. That is why I do not recommend "The Pep Talk" to everyone, mainly because it requires the trainer to practice all that he preaches and to be a great example. Sadly, this does not always occur.

All things must be done in moderation with new missionaries. Some move fast, others move slowly. Some speak the foreign language well coming out of the MTC, and others take months to grasp the language. Some are totally focused and others just can't seem to get their head in the ball game. That is what being a trainer is all about, pushing your companion (as well as yourself) just enough to challenge him, but not to break him.

Inventory meeting. After you have had "the talk" with your new companion, and he has had a good night is sleep, it is important that you two sit down and set many goals in your first inventory meeting. Do not wait until your first P-Day to have this meeting with your new companion. It is necessary that you two are on the same wavelength right from the beginning. In your first inventory meeting, you should talk about goals regarding your area and as well as personal goals with respect to your companion's level of certification, discussions, and scriptures. Make sure that you both participate in this meeting, and that your companion, taking your suggestions into consideration, does most of his own goal setting for his personal studies.

Such an inventory meeting is imperative each week during training (as well as the rest of your mission). During these meetings, give your companion the opportunity to vent any frustrations that he may be having. If he says that he does not have any, you may ask a few questions just to be sure. Almost always, new missionaries need to vent about certain things, and that is why trainers must sometimes help their companions talk about their feelings. This way all problems will be resolved before they become major difficulties. Also, before you give your companion constructive criticism, find out what *you* could be doing better. After doing these things and discussing your area, you will then be able set goals to improve your effectiveness as missionaries.

These inventory meetings can only be effective if each missionary is humble. As a trainer, you must realize that you are not perfect and that you, too, can improve on many things. Always ask your greenie what he thinks you could do better to help him. Look at and treat him as an equal to yourself and I promise you that you will both be mutually edified.

Do all that you can to help your new missionary improve his proselyting skills rapidly. Here are some suggestions:

—Practice repeating the discussions while walking in the street.

—With regards to learning a new language, have your companion conjugate and translate verbs and sentences that you give him, using constant repetition.

—At the right moment, correct your companion if he messes up with regards to the language, and have him do the same for you.

—Study the in-field together everyday!

—Do role-playing activities in your apartments and in the street to become better prepared for anything that your companion may encounter.

—Give feedback to each other after each house that you go in.

These are just a few suggestions of what you and your new missionary can do to help each other be the best that you can be. I have done each one of them and I have a strong testimony that each one works. If you have enough humility and diligence, I know you will find the same to be true.

Give him the ball. It was not until I was made a senior companion that I was actually able to challenge someone to be baptized. This was because all of my senior companions had chosen to do the challenges themselves, leaving me unprepared for what lay ahead. Having gone through this, I made sure that each one of the missionaries that I trained was very experienced in numbers of discussions that they had taught as well as the people they had committed to baptism. In fact, once I felt that the time had come, I would have my greenies teach the entire first discussion by themselves. I would only bear my testimony and reiterate when I felt it was necessary. The act of teaching an entire first discussion gives a new missionary resounding confidence. I had many great experiences as a trainer that reinforced this idea.

Once I was called to continue the training of a missionary who had just completed his first month in the mission field. His first companion, although a tremendous missionary, had not let him teach much during the discussions. After being together for about a week with this new missionary, we found ourselves teaching the first discussion in the house of a wonderful lady. I let my companion teach the first principle, and then after teaching it, he looked at me (as missionaries always do) so that I would pick up with the second principle. But instead of teaching it, I let him "have the ball," and told him to continue. Again, after the second principle, he looked at me so that I would teach, but I immediately nodded back to him, which meant that he was to continue. By this point he realized that something was up. He grinned a little, proceeded to teach, and finished the rest of the discussion. Despite his struggles with the language, he had done a wonderful job. I knew that the lady (who was eventually baptized) was prepared to hear our message, and it would be the perfect opportunity for my "son" to get some experience and confidence.

I can vividly remember leaving that little house that day and the joy that I felt as my companion leaped in the air. He was so thrilled with his achievement that he gave me a big hug, and then proceeded to thank me about ten times for having given him the chance to teach the entire discussion. He had so yearned for such an opportunity, and because I had faith in his abilities he was able to feel like a real missionary and experience overwhelming joy.

With each one of the missionaries I trained, I looked for every opportunity to "give them the ball" and in doing so, they were able to progress faster than most other missionaries who had the same amount of time as they did in the mission field. At times, trainers feel that the only way in which they will have success with investigators is to do almost all of the teaching themselves. This is absolutely false. New missionaries have just as much power and potential as a missionary who has two years in the field. I promise you that you will never lose a true investigator because of the teaching or technical faults of your companion. You can only benefit from their teachings.

Another way to get your companion involved is to have him plan with you in all that you do as a companionship. You can even have your companion plan an entire evening or morning by himself. This experience will help him to be more in tuned with all that is going on in your area and it will also give him needed experience for what lies ahead in the rest of his mission.

Learn! I mentioned at the start of this chapter that I learned a great amount from the new missionaries that I had the opportunity to train. In fact, I feel I learned much more from them than they learned from me. I have listed the five missionaries that I was able to train and what I learned from each.

Elder Erickson: This elder taught me the importance of always having a good spirit in the discussions. When I was young in my mission, I had the tendency to try and prove people wrong when teaching the gospel. As you have probably heard, this teaching style does not convert. Elder Erickson noticed this and helped me to change my approach. He also helped me a great deal with the Spanish language. Although I could converse with the language better than he could at that time, he was much better with his pronunciation and accent than I was, which was very beneficial to me. We would constantly correct each other, but we had an understanding that it was for our better, and so we both benefited.

Elder Stock: This wonderful young man taught me about love and the need to have love for the people in order to have success with missionary work. He was quite a thinker, and was thus very creative in his work, which made me also try to be creative.

Elder Clark: Elder Clark kept us working all of the time.

He loved his mission and could not have cared less about anything else. From day one he was talking to anyone he possibly could in the street, even though he struggled with the language at first like all new missionaries. He had no fear, and I fed off this mentality.

Elder Smith: He was the most humble man that I have ever met. Elder Smith was always analyzing himself in order to improve on his weaknesses. Being in his presence made me feel like I was with the Savior. Elder Smith also studied his discussions so much in the street that it gave me a headache. I would always ask myself, "Does this guy ever quit studying?!" He never took a break or wasted a second. He was relentless in his pursuit of perfection, which was quite a humbling experience.

Elder Burton: This elder had gone to church as a teenager his whole life without the companionship of his parents and family, who were all inactive Church members. Because of his great faith and diligence, his parents made it back to the temple right before he left on his mission. Elder Burton was a living example of how one member of a family can take charge and lift everyone else around him.

I could say much more about what I learned from these wonderful young men, but I will not. It suffices me to say that they were a special group and they helped mold me into the man that I am today through their amazing example of living the gospel. There is no reason why you cannot experience the same.

As always, love is your key. As a trainer, you can do everything that I have suggested in this chapter, but it will all be for nothing if you do not learn to love your junior companion. Love is such a healer when it comes to companionships. When I think about just how much those five young men changed my life, and also the experiences that we lived through together, tears come to my eyes. The bonds that you will form with certain companions while out in the mission field are like no other friendships that you have experienced up to this point. The conversion of souls does not only link the missionary and the investigator, but also forms an indescribable bond with the two missionaries that laughed, prayed, sang, worked, and cried to make such a conversion possible.

I sincerely hope that you will also form eternal friendships during your missionary service with the companions that you will have. Words do not give justice to the feelings that I have for the missionaries that I trained as we attempted to reap the harvest of souls that were prepared for us.

Chapter Seven:

Obedience

All the water in the world cannot sink the smallest ship unless it gets inside.—Boyd K. Packer

Most every missionary preparation book has a chapter dealing with the important aspect of obedience, and how it affects all facets of one's success in the field. This book will be no different. I wish I could somehow show you just how exact obedience in your mission will be of great benefit to you, but I cannot. You will have to experience this on your own. I can only share with you my own experiences dealing with obedience and what I learned about it as I served the Lord.

Upon arriving in the mission field in Chile, the mission president told me that although the amounts of convert baptisms that the mission had were very important to him, the most important responsibility that he had was to help ensure the individual conversion of the missionaries that served under him. He wanted to be sure that, regardless of whether a missionary had five or five hundred baptisms in his mission, he would be active in the church twenty years down the road. I was surprised to hear such a statement from my mission president. I knew that he cared about his missionaries, but I had no idea that he took their spiritual progress so seriously. That day, I realized that before I was to worry about baptizing all of southern Chile, I had to be sure that the habits I formed while in the mission field would, first of all, be eternally beneficial to me, and then the rest would take care of itself.

Before arriving in the mission field, I was under the opinion that all a missionary had to do in order to baptize many people was work hard and be completely obedient to mission rules. However, once I had been out in the field for a short time, I realized otherwise. I was surprised to see that some missionaries, who were not very obedient, seemed to baptize more than many of their most obedient peers. I often wondered why this was. After I became more experienced in the field, I came to a few realizations: I realized that the number of baptisms that a missionary has is based on a number of variables, including: faith, testimony, hard work, prayer, obedience, the will of the Father, techniques, and many others. This being said, you can see that obedience is just one of many elements which contribute to the effectiveness of a missionary.

Despite the fact that obedience does not always lead to huge numbers of baptisms on a missionary's part, it does lead to the individual conversion of that missionary. This should be the number one goal of your mission. If you work to convert and entrench yourself in the gospel while you labor for eighteen or twenty four months, you will have to be obedient, and the only way to be obedient is to be a hard worker, which will in turn greatly increase the probability that you will have success in seeing many souls enter into the waters of baptism.

I hope that you read this and understand what I am trying to point out. From an eternal perspective, if you do not train yourself to be obedient to the laws of the gospel, the amount of conversions that you may reach in your mission are without significance. Only accept the best from yourself. I know that the rules that your mission president gives are inspired of God. Do not question his decisions. Also, do not compromise the missionary handbook. The Doctrine and Covenants section 130 teaches us that every rule and act of obedience that you have will lead to greater blessings. I have tasted the truthfulness of this promise many times, especially while out in the mission field.

At one point in my mission, I had been recently called as a zone leader. The zone that I was called to serve in was one of the poorest zones in the mission with respect to number of baptisms each month. After my first two weeks in the zone, we did not have any baptisms among all of the companionships. I was greatly stressed and bothered by this fact, but I hoped that we could turn things around during the last two weeks of the month.

During this time period when the zone was struggling, we decided to go on an outing as a zone and see a waterfall and a few of the other beautiful sites that that part of Chile had to offer. Therefore, one P-Day we all got together and left on a long ride to see the waterfall and other attractions. These attractions were located a few hours away by van, so we had to move quickly to get everything accomplished and to make it back in time in order to leave our areas at 6:00 and proselyte. We ended up leaving a bit late that morning and as we toured the different sites, the day seemed to shorten quickly.

Throughout the day, I had to remind everyone to hurry so that we would have enough time to see the waterfall, but most missionaries just kept their same pace, which caused me to worry. Finally, it was almost three o'clock in the afternoon and we still had not seen the waterfall. We were all in the van traveling back to our starting point where we would stop by the waterfall and then catch buses to get back to our areas before 6:00. As I was riding in the van, thinking about how the zone would be late if we stopped to see the waterfall, I realized that there was no way that we were going to make it. We had two choices, go to the waterfall and get back late, or go directly to the bus stop in order to make it back just on time. I decided that we had no choice. We would go back and skip the water-fall.

After telling everyone in the van what my plan was, I realized that I was in the minority. In fact, my two district leaders, who are a zone leader's main support in his zone, were in complete disagreement with me. Everyone in the van was frustrated, and other than my own companion, I felt all alone. I could not believe that my zone, despite not having baptized anyone for the first two weeks of the month, did not want to make it back to their areas on time. While I was thinking about ways in which my companionship could receive blessings by being obedient, they were thinking about waterfalls. After arguing about whether we would see the waterfall or skip it, I eventually said that there was no debate on the subject and we would get back to work as soon as possible. Needless to say, the rest of that two-hour ride back was a very long trip. I felt like everyone was talking about me and my heart was struck with sadness.

That night, after having returned from proselyting, I was still so distraught that I decided to call the mission president and seek counsel from him. He, too, was irritated and decided to send his two assistants to my zone in order to work with the missionaries and straighten things up.

The following day, one of the assistants, Elder Airmet, came to work with me in my area while my companion worked in another area for that day. Elder Airmet had been a missionary in my area before I had gotten there. We went around to some of his old investigators, including a family of five that he had worked with for six months previously, and who had almost gotten baptized but just lacked a little extra motivation. I had talked with them a few times with no real progress. Despite being regulars at church, something was holding them back. Elder Airmet told me that he wanted to challenge them to be baptized again, and so we had to work together to help them feel the Spirit strong enough to accept. That is exactly what happened. We met with the family and challenged them to be baptized, and the spirit was undeniable. The whole family accepted and all were baptized the next day in a beautiful lake with volcanoes in the background. It was a very special day, and the pictures that I took of that family all dressed in white are highlights of my missionary experience. I know that that family would not have gotten baptized if it were not for the elder who was with me. He is the one who had the relationship of trust with them. I feel that Heavenly Father wanted us together that day in order for this family to accept such a difficult commitment.

To close this story, by the end of that month, my companion and I had been able to see six wonderful souls enter into the waters of baptism. A sister companionship in the zone, who had not gone on the waterfall outing, had also baptized a man from a part-member family with the help of the other assistant. The rest of the zone had not baptized anyone.

I hope that upon reading the events of this story, you can see the domino effect that obedience, as well as disobedience, has on the success of a missionary. Think for a minute. If I had given in to the wishes of the missionaries in my zone that day, we would all have been late. If I had been late, I probably would not have called the mission president that night. Without such a call, the assistants would never have come to my zone to help, and I would never have been able to challenge that wonderful family with the help of Elder Airmet, who had gone through so much to help them get baptized in the first place. The sisters were blessed because they had not participated in the problems dealing with the P-Day activity. I believe that the man whom they were able to see baptized would not have accepted baptism if it were not for the great assistant who helped them.

The rest of the zone had no "fruits" that month, and the reasons for this are obvious.

This is one of the greatest and clearest examples that I have seen of the promise that the Lord gives us in Doctrine and Covenants 130:21. We must first obey, and then we shall obtain. I learned so much from that experience as a zone leader. The Lord will at times give us obvious blessings if we do his will.

I also learned that focus is a critical aspect of being a great missionary. Remember, a mission is not about what we do on P-Day, it is about what we do the rest of the week. I also learned that at times, we must go against the majority to do what is right, even in the mission field. I could relay stories of obedience all day, but I believe that my point has been made.

This experience helped me grow as a person and as a missionary. I do not claim to never have made wrong decisions in my mission, nor am I here to say that I was any more righteous than those elders and sisters whom I was with that day, but one thing that I am absolutely sure of is that it pays to be obedient. It pays to follow the big rules and the little rules. Without such a commitment to follow the Lord's will, the Spirit will not reside in the missionary, and failure will undoubtedly occur.

Commit yourself to being the most obedient missionary that you can be. You will accomplish this not by what you say, but by the actions that you take. Promise yourself that you will not have any regrets after your missionary service, and I know that it will work. I love the commandments. I appreciate the fact that we are guided by the Lord as to what we are supposed to be doing as missionaries. Such commandments are not really commandments, but rather opportunities to receive the fullness of blessings that are awaiting us as well as the people that we come in contact with.

Chapter Eight:

Leadership

"Your biggest challenge isn't someone else. It's the ache in your lungs and the burning in your legs, and the voice inside you that yells 'CAN'T', but you don't listen. You just push harder. And then you hear the voice whisper 'can'. And you discover that the person you thought you were is no match for the one you really are." — *Unknown*

Junior companion, senior companion, trainer, district leader, zone leader, and assistant to the president: I'm sure that you have heard of all of these titles. They are, of course, the callings that one can receive in the mission field. I imagine that you have also heard of missionaries who have sought to reach such positions. Sadly enough, such is the case all too often in the mission field. Despite this fact, this does not mean that you should strive to do the same. Missionaries are so much more respected when they worry only about the calling that they have, and not about a calling that they would hope to hold. I do not want to talk much about the subject of position-seeking in the mission field. I can only hope that you will do that which you already know to be right—performing your calling with all of your heart, might, mind, and strength. The rest will just take care of itself. I promise you that if you do choose unwisely, your leadership abilities will be much less effective in the mission field because your peers will see the truth.

Now, getting past the ugly part, I would like to say that every calling in the mission has an unlimited amount of potential in regards to how it can help the progression of an elder or sister. Frankly, I loved helping and leading missionaries when I was called to do so in my mission. It gave me such a sense of joy when I was able to boost the morale of and help another missionary. Anyone who serves a mission has the capability to do so with the utmost effectiveness and success. Therefore, when your time comes to hold a certain position in field (if that is the Lord's will), I hope you will expound on and magnify it to the greatest degree possible. Even if the Lord sees fit that you serve as a junior companion for your whole mission, I know that you can still lead just as many missionaries by setting the proper example. Your potential as a leader is unlimited. I hope that you will start to see this potential while out in the mission field. The choice is yours.

Zone leader. It can be difficult to be a leader in the mission field. With leadership comes responsibilities, and with these responsibilities usually come stress and a heavier workload. When I was first called to be a zone leader in my mission, I felt rather lost as to how exactly I was to run my zone. I had never served with a zone leader previously, and as in most missions, I basically had to learn what to do on my own without much training. I'm not sure if I was ever a great zone leader or not, but I have listed some suggestions to help anyone who is just beginning to serve as a zone leader, or even a district leader. Also, whether you become a zone leader or not in your mission, I know that the following suggestions can be beneficial to your missionary experience.

Suggestions for running a zone

—Upon receiving your calling, pray about your zone and how you should run it. Pray about the individual needs of each missionary and what you can do to help each person reach his potential.

—When you meet with your zone for the first time, make sure that everyone takes the time to introduce himself so that you can begin to know each missionary in your zone. Be sure to gain the respect of your fellow missionaries before you begin to offer too many suggestions on how the missionaries can improve their successes. Also, in this first meeting, explain to your zone members how often you are going to call them, the possibility of splits, goals, and other plans. This way, there will be no surprises.

—Make sure that many members of your zone participate in the zone meetings. Help everyone to contribute to these meetings and when you set goals (which should take place in every meeting), be sure to do it as a zone. This will help you to be more consecrated. One major key to helping your fellow missionaries reach certain goals is to make sure that the goals are theirs, not yours. No matter how righteous and inspired you may feel about a certain goal, if a companionship does not have their heart in it, they will almost undoubtedly fail. Your job is to stimulate and motivate. By doing this, the missionaries in your zone will be sure to set high standards and then do all that is possible to reach them.

—Your zone meetings must be an uplifting and spiritual experience. Your missionaries should leave from these meetings with a clear idea of what the meeting accomplished, and also how they are going to reach the goals that have been set. Prepare these meetings well so that they are organized and run smoothly. It is usually very ineffective to "shoot from the hip," and your missionaries will see your ineptitude.

—Be the most enthusiastic missionary that you can possibly be! Strive to have enthusiasm among all of the missionaries in your zone. Do not accept a lackadaisical attitude toward the work. If you see this in your missionaries, help them feel the powers of enthusiasm through your fired-up excitement. Remember, it all   starts with you.

—Put yourself on the same level as the missionaries whom you deal with. Acknowledge that you, too, are not perfect and be humble! This will help the members of your zone to open up to you more.

—If possible, call your district leaders every day, and make sure that they talk to the members of their district daily also. When having these conversations, continue to spend a little time getting to know and show genuine love for each member of your zone. Not every conversation needs to, nor should it, deal with numbers. Focus more on inspiration and positive thoughts rather than numbers.

—As a zone leader, delegate. You are wrong to try to get all of the attention. The best zone leaders are the ones who know how to get the most out of their district leaders.

—Be creative! It often takes an imagination to get a zone fired up. You are entitled to such revelation.

—Do splits often. This will help the missionaries form a stronger bond among themselves and also they will be more aware of what is going on in the areas of the rest of the zone. Splits are also very critical because they enable you, as the zone leader, to really know what is going on in the different areas of your zone instead of just hearing about it. This is the best verification that you could possibly have as a zone leader. Splits are worth more than ten phone calls. I cannot stress their importance enough.

—Have missionaries earnestly pray for each other and their investigators.

—Take the responsibility to see that each companionship in your zone will baptize monthly. If that means that you do splits in every area of your zone to ensure such success, then so be it. You should be just as worried for the success of each companionship in your zone as you are for your own success.

—Create a "model" area. Bring in other missionaries so that they can see the success that you are having and learn of how you are having it.

—Don't be afraid to ask for help, especially from the assistants and the mission president. That is what they are there for.

—Know that each missionary is motivated in different ways. Again, it is your responsibility to find out what these ways are.

—Being negative or degrading to any missionary will never bring about positive results. In fact, it will destroy any relationship of trust that you may already have. If a missionary has done poorly or made a bad decision in some way, he almost always is already aware of their actions. No one needs to be kicked when they are down. Be lavish in your praise and constant in your approbation.

—Love your missionaries with all your heart. If you have ill feeling toward any missionary in your zone, talk with that person until you have positive feelings for each other. Do not allow any hard feelings to affect you or the rest of the missionaries in your zone.

I am sure that there are a thousand more good suggestions with regards to running a zone, but I feel that if anyone can master these, they will have an incredible amount of success. Every zone leader has his own ideas and is distinct from others, as well he should be. I know that the opportunity that one receives when called to this position is a great learning opportunity and should be treated as such.

To close, I would remind you to give all that you have to whatever calling that may come your way while in the mission. Don't hurt yourself and others by attempting to destine a future that you cannot control. The future is in the Lord's hands.

Chapter Nine:

Inviting the Spirit to the Discussions

In the coming chapters, I am going to talk about teaching techniques to be used in the discussions. But first, it is imperative that we talk about how you can create an environment in your discussions that will be conducive to the spirit.

When I was baptized, I knew very little about the doctrine of the gospel. Even though I was a senior in high school when I received the discussions, the message of the missionaries was so new and complex that I only picked up certain points. The important thing is that what I learned from the missionaries is not the reason for my decision to be baptized, but rather the feelings that I experienced as I was taught the fullness of the gospel for the first time.

I tell this story because when someone is learning about the gospel for the first time, it is very difficult to remember most of the details of the discussions. Everyone varies in the degree of what they can comprehend and remember from the discussions, but as a whole, the majority of your investigators will need to hear the principles of the discussions many times in order to grasp all of their teachings. This is one reason why we have new-member discussions. Having said this, I would like to point out that the one thing that all new converts should remember is the feeling of sitting in a room, receiving the gospel, and having the Spirit indicate to them that what they are hearing is true. In order for this to be possible, a missionary must do everything possible to invite the Spirit to the discussions. In your mission, you will understand more than ever just how sensitive the Spirit is and how fast it can enter or leave your discussions.

I testify that the environment of the discussions will often be the most deciding factor in whether or not a person can feel the Spirit and therefore have a spiritual conversion to the gospel.

When I chose to talk with the elders for the first time, we decided to take the discussions in the house of a friend of mine who was a member, which is a very blessed and special house to me. It was always kept very clean, never cluttered. There were pictures of Christ and temples hanging on the walls. The air had a becoming scent to it, and more than anything, it was a relaxed environment. There were never any distractions during the discussions. The two elders and I would just sit in a room of this house and talk away about life and the Plan of Salvation.

Just the thought of sitting with those two spiritual giants in that lovely setting brings a smile to my face. There was something so special about those moments. Still to this day, I cherish that time period in my life. I know that if I had not felt such strong feelings in my friend's house, I would not have had the courage to be baptized. I can say this because, just as Joseph Smith could not deny that he had seen a vision, I could not deny that the feelings that I experienced with the elders were of God. I also feel that we could not have had the same success in regards to feeling the spirit in my own house. It was a paradox to the house aforementioned.

The atmosphere that I have just described is what you need to strive for in all of your discussions. Granted, such a setting is unrealistic in all cases, but it is still very often conceivable. This is why it is so critical that you strive to teach discussions to non-members in the houses of members. The sacrifice that it takes to plan such an environment will pay off tenfold. I know this because it worked with me and it also worked with many of the wonderful people that I was able to teach in Chile.

Now that we have established that the atmosphere of a discussion is important, I would like to offer a few more suggestions that will help you to set the tone of the discussions and make them as spiritual as possible.

Never teach when the TV is on. If a person insists on leaving it on while you are in the house, just tell them that you will come back at another time. This applies to radios, screaming children, and other noise. If you elect to teach a discussion with such distractions, your teachings will be in vain. Teaching just to say that you taught a discussion is futile and will not help you fulfill your calling or bring people unto Christ.

Do your best to teach the discussions at a table if possible. This is important for a variety of reasons: First of all, it helps all participants of the discussion to be more involved and active in the conversation. Secondly, it keeps anyone from getting sleepy and nodding off, which is a common occurrence among missionaries, especially when they have had little time in the field. Although couches and chairs will do, I have found that teaching at a table is the most effective method.

Upon entering into a house for the first time, take the time to get to know the people, especially the head of the household. If you show interest in your investigators, they will be more likely to open up to you and take interest in your message. We will talk about this in depth later.

Although children can greatly enhance the spirituality of a discussion, they can also wreak havoc. It is next to impossible to feel the Spirit when there is a kid screaming because he wants to play with Mommy. A missionary once suggested to me to bring small jigsaw puzzles to the discussions to give the children a novel item to play with. I followed his advice and it worked.

Be sure to invite all of the people in the house to participate in the discussion. Often, people want to participate in the
discussions but don't feel invited, and so therefore they stay in
another room. Be sure that you ask if all members of the family
who are at home would like to participate.

There are other steps that can be taken to ensure that
every environment that you teach in as a missionary, is
conducive to the spirit. I have just listed a few of them, but I
hope that you will do your best to follow the suggestions that I
have given in this chapter. Make sure your investigators feel
the same I did during my discussions with the elders, because
it is a feeling that they will never be able to forget.

Chapter Ten:

The First Discussion

The happiest missionaries in the world are the ones who find themselves always teaching. Our duty is to teach the gospel and bring people unto Christ through his saving ordinances.

I have written this chapter to help you to get a clearer vision of the first discussion, how it was written, and what you can do to help your investigators to really grasp its teachings. I feel that these suggestions will help you if you apply them, but I also realize that every missionary has a distinct style of teaching the first discussion. I changed the manner in which I taught the first discussion many times while I was out in the mission field. I think that it is important that a missionary evolves as a teacher. This means that you are constantly improving your techniques and abilities to better preach the gospel. If you find that you teach the same first discussion the first month of your mission as you do in the last month of your mission, chances are that you have not developed very well. Take pride in your evolution as a missionary.

Setting the path of the discussions. Before we analyze the first discussion, I want to mention that there are many "find out" questions that you will see listed in the coming chapters which to some people might be considered manipulative. I want it to be clear to you that there is a very obvious difference between teaching via manipulation, and teaching via leading. A "find out" question that leads is one that stimulates the thoughts of an investigator and helps them to progress spiritually. Let me give you an example. Here in this chapter, I mention that a very good question to ask your investigators with regards to Joseph Smith is:

"Mr. John, why would it be important for you to find out if Joseph Smith was a prophet?"

Some people may consider this question to be manipulative. To that person, I would then ask a common, everyday question, something like:

"Jack, why is it important that you go to college?"

Would this also then be considered manipulative? Of course not, mainly because it helps Jack to contemplate his future and his need to attend college.

The question about Joseph Smith helps Mr. John to think about why he needs to know if Joseph Smith was a prophet. It is our goal as missionaries to teach the discussions and ask questions to reach the investigators on a personal level, so that they can contemplate the effect of the gospel in their own lives. Questions that do not lead to personal thought by the investigators are not very effective.

Now I will give an example of manipulation:

"Mr. John, as you can read here in the Bible, if we love the Savior, then we should obey his commandments. Therefore, if you really do love the Savior, will you follow his commandments and be baptized in His church?"

This is a perfect example of manipulation. Such attempts to persuade do not invite the Spirit, and should never be used by missionaries of the Lord's Church.

I hope that you can see the difference between the two teaching techniques. One is good, and the other is bad. One involves the spirit, and the other does not. One helps the investigator to think for himself, and the other does not allow for personal contemplation.

Setting the spiritual tone of the discussion. Before beginning the first principle of the first discussion, I have found that it is important to do a few things in order to set the spiritual tone of the lesson. After you have built a relationship of trust with your listeners, be sure that they understand fully who you are, your testimony about the message that you are sharing, and the purpose of your presence in their home. I would usually say something to this effect:

Missionary: "We truly are representatives of the Savior Jesus Christ and he has sent us here to help your family know the fulness of his gospel. As missionaries, we share discussions with people to help them understand what our church believes. Upon hearing this message, they can know if the church is the true church of Jesus Christ and can therefore decide if they would like to become members."

"For this reason, we would like to invite you to listen intently to the message which we are about to share and to try to feel in your hearts if it is true. These feelings are what are more commonly known as the Holy Spirit. In fact, Paul tells us in Ephesians how we can tell if the Spirit is touching us. (read Ephesians 5:22.) If you have such feelings during our message, you will then be able to know if the wonderful things that we are telling you are true."

"Mr. Black, upon reading this part of the Bible, how will you know if our message is true?"

Mr. Black: "I will feel it in my heart."

Missionary: "Excellent, that is exactly how you will know. And what are some of the feelings that you could have?"

Mr. Black: "Love and peace."

Missionary: "Great! It sounds like you understand perfectly how you and your family can know if this message is true. Before we start, we would like to have a word of prayer..."

Now, this is one of a million possible introductions for your first discussion, but I hope you can see what is accomplished if a missionary takes a few seconds to say these things:

—The family understands your calling.

—Upon bearing your testimony, you will be able to better invite the spirit, thus setting the tone of the discussion.

—Because you have stated your purpose for being there, the investigators will either try to find out if the message is true or tell you point blank that they are not willing to open up to what you have to say. If such is the case, and the people in the house tell you that they refuse to open their hearts to your message, the best thing that you can do is leave and thank them for their honesty. This will keep you from wasting forty-five minutes of the Lord's time and help you to maximize every second that you have.

—By explaining what the Spirit is before starting the discussion, your investigators will immediately see how they are to know the truth. Also, the Spirit is what really converts a non-member to the gospel, and so the more that you can explain it as a missionary, the better chance that your investigators will be apt to identify it. By explaining the fruits of the Spirit before starting the discussion, you will talk about the Holy Ghost at least three times by the end of the first discussion.

Great! We have set the tone and now we must teach. Again I remind you that each person is different, and so therefore each first discussion needs to be individualized. The example that I am about to give applies mainly to people who are Christians. I have found that most Christians will believe in God, His Son, and in the Holy Spirit in some shape or form. Although now more than ever there is an incredible range of beliefs in the world, most of the very basic beliefs are shared. I would give you an example of how to teach the first discussion to an atheist or a Buddhist, but that would take the fun out of it for you. Like I said earlier; there exist so many different ways and methods to teach the discussions, I could write an entire book on that one subject.

It is important that you understand as a missionary the need to really comprehend what the discussions are trying to get across to the listener and also how they were written. The first discussion is like a chain of many links connected to form an incredibly strong bond. I compare the first discussion (and all of the discussions) to a chain, and the principles of the discussion are its links. Now, what happens if you try to pull a truck using a chain and one of its links is broken? Obviously, the chain will snap and be completely ineffective just because one link out of many was defective. Just as the link of a chain may determine its ability to withstand pressure, the principles of the discussions are closely interrelated, and if an investigator does not understand one principle, the whole discussion will likely be ineffective.

Remember this when you are teaching the discussions, especially the first one: If a person thinks that a "prophet" has the same authority as a priest or preacher, then principle number four, which claims that Joseph Smith was a prophet, has no significance to the listener. Continuing with this thought, if your investigator does not understand Joseph Smith's role as a prophet, then his translation of the Book of Mormon in principle number five will also be of little value to the investigator. Each principle of the first discussion is dependent on all of the previous principles. Also, each principle leads and prepares the investigator to hear the following one. You must learn to develop a fluidness in your discussions. Upon doing so, your investigators will be greatly enlightened and will therefore be converted more often.

Principle One: Our Heavenly Father's Plan

I can only give a few tips of advice with regards to this principle:

—Keep it short—The more time you spend with the first principle, the less time you have for the final three.

—Ask only one question if possible. Again, this mainly has to do with time, but it also has to do with efficiency as a missionary.

Many missionaries ask two questions while teaching the first principle, which go something like this:
"Mr. Franks, what are your feelings about God?"
"Mr. Franks, what do you feel knowing that God has a plan for you and your family?"
I feel that your goal as a missionary teaching the first principle should be to explain that, as children of God, Heavenly Father has a plan of happiness for all of us. You need to help the investigator to start thinking about the joy that your message will bring to his life. After all, doesn't everyone want to be happy? Of course! And you are their ticket to true and eternal happiness! That is why I suggest that you complete the first principle with this question:
"Mr. Franks, what feelings do you have knowing that your Father in Heaven has provided an eternal plan of happiness for you and for your family?"

This question will serve these purposes:

—The investigator will immediately say if he believes in God or not, thus letting you find out what they feel about God early on in the principle without having to ask another question.

—It is not a yes or no question, which is clearly ineffective.

—It makes the head of the household feel important when you mention the word "you" four times in the question. People yearn to feel important. Men, more than anything, like others to recognize their authority in the home. This question fulfills both needs.

—When you ask someone what "feelings" they have for something, you are giving them an opportunity to reflect and therefore feel the Spirit. These two actions are what convert people to the gospel.

—You will see if the investigator understands the principle just taught.

Actually, I could continue but I think the point has been made. If you teach the principle the way it is written and ask this question, you will be sailing into the second principle. You now know that the investigator wants to be happy. This is key because the second principle shows him how he can be happy— by following the precepts of Jesus Christ. (Can you see the links start to form?)

Principle Two: The divine Sonship of Christ

Like the first principle, the second is relatively basic. I

feel that the most important goal of the second principle is to have the investigator feel the need to follow the Savior and His example. In paragraph four of the principle, we read:

"The plan of salvation is simple and easy to understand, but we must choose to follow it." This statement is probably the most important of the principle. I say this because not many people will remember after the first discussion how Christ helped us to overcome sin and death. That is why we have the second discussion. What investigators need to grasp in the first discussion is that the plan of salvation, or the message that you are sharing, is simple and easy to understand, but we must choose to follow it.

Upon saying this, you are bringing up the principle of free agency for the first time to your investigators. The only way that they can be converted to the gospel is if they choose to follow the teachings of the discussions. It is imperative that they feel this need. It is your job to help them want to make such a commitment.

Also, a major point of the principle is the next "link." In Principle One we talked about our search for happiness; and in Principle Two we talked about how Christ is our means whereby we can find such happiness. If the investigators desire to follow Christ and his teachings, we now must show them how they can accomplish such. The answer is through the help of prophets, which, of course, is Principle Three.

Here are a few more tips from the second principle:

—Just as in the first principle, try to keep it short. You will need to save the time for later.

—You have a great chance to bring in the spirit to the discussion as you bear testimony of the Savior. Take advantage of this moment and do everything under your power to invite the warmth of the Holy Ghost.

There are tons of questions that can be asked in Principle Two. Take the time to come up with as many questions as possible and then apply them to your discussions. Here are a few that your discussion booklet does not give:

—How does Christ affect your life?

—Why would it be important that we follow the teachings of Christ?

—How can the act of following the Savior's example help you in your life?

Principle Three: How the plan has been revealed

This principle is very important to the success of the first discussion because it sets the tone for the story of Joseph Smith. I have seen many missionaries (including myself) teach this principle poorly, which leads to problems and misunderstandings in Principle Four. In order to make the teaching of this principle as effective as possible, here are a few suggestions:

—The key to making sure that the investigator understands the role of a prophet is to ask questions. When explaining what a prophet is, I have found that the best "find out" question that can be asked is, "What is the difference between a prophet and a priest or a preacher?"

—This question is helpful because the investigator will be able to understand that a prophet is much more inspired and righteous than other leaders of their own faith. Your investigators must comprehend that a prophet has authority that no other man on earth has. Often in my mission, when I would ask this question, the investigator would say that there was no difference between their preacher and a prophet. Whenever I heard this, I knew I had to re-teach about the profound role and authority of a prophet. If you do not ask this question, many of your investigators will think that Joseph Smith was just a good man who had faith just like their local preachers.

—Ensure that the investigators understand how the Holy Spirit works in telling us that a prophet, or a message, is true. You can never talk too much about how the Lord reveals his truths. More often than not, missionaries do not spend enough time explaining the Holy Ghost, which causes the investigators to misinterpret promptings that may come to them.

—Like all of the principles of the first discussion, a question is needed to help the discussion, as well as the investigator's mindset, flow into the story of Joseph Smith. I have found that the best question to achieve this transition is: Why would it be important that there was a prophet of the Lord in this time period?

Of course, there are various ways in which this question can be asked, but the main idea should always be the same. When a person hears this question and has understood what a prophet is, they will almost always say something like this:
"It would probably help the people to have more faith," or, "It would clear up a lot of questions with respect to the Bible."
When an investigator answers in this manner, he is

preparing himself to understand the profound calling and mission of Joseph Smith. This is what you want to accomplish. Upon hearing such a response, you should always respond with an emphatic "yes"! Your goal should be to get your investigators excited about the fact that someone has been called in these days to lead us out of confusion and into the truth that so many people yearn to have.

Remember, all of these questions and techniques are of no value if you are not full of enthusiasm during the discussion. You must light a fire in whatever setting you may find yourself teaching in.

Principle Four: The Prophet Joseph Smith

The first three principles of the first discussion basically expound on the similar beliefs that we have in the Church of Jesus Christ of Latter-day Saints with the majority of the other Christian churches in the world today. After these principles have been taught, we break away from this pattern and begin to explain new truths that the rest of the religious world has yet to learn and accept.

Here are a few of my suggestions about the fourth principle:

If there is any part of the first discussion that you can use your own words effectively it would be in this principle. I would exhort you to just talk to your investigators and explain to them as you would to a friend about the confusion the young Joseph had as a boy and what he did to find the truth. This needs to be one of the spiritual high points of the first discussion. To make this plausible, you must, as a missionary, feel the Spirit before your investigators can feed off your spirit. If you say the same thing and use the same questions with every discussion, you will likely struggle to feel the Spirit as strongly as you could.

Therefore, be creative and excited every time you talk about Joseph Smith and you will see wonderful results.

With regards to Joseph Smith's account of the first vision, many missionaries do not show the picture (found in the missionary flipcharts) of young Joseph praying for an answer. Other missionaries show the picture of Joseph praying, and then they show another picture of Joseph looking up at God the Father and His Son. Personally, when I received the first discussion from the missionaries, afterwards I remembered very little . But I do remember my feelings of excitement when the missionaries showed me the flipchart picture of Joseph faithfully praying. That image has always stuck with me, so I would admonish all missionaries to use visual aids whenever possible, especially when giving an account of the first vision.

You will find that most of the conversions that you will have in your mission will come from the times when you are not in the home of the investigator. This is because, just like Enos' experience in contemplating the teachings of his father, when an investigator contemplates and ponders the teachings of a missionary, he is much more likely to be struck by the influence of the spirit and be converted to the gospel. Visual aids help to spawn contemplative thoughts in your investigators.

Understand that more often than not, your investigators will have doubts about Joseph Smith after hearing his story for the first time. This is fine. It took Brigham Young two years to be baptized, so it is okay if someone has doubts, it is to be expected. And that is why, after bearing your testimony about Joseph Smith and finding out what they felt upon hearing his story, you should ask a question. I would suggest something like this:

"Mr. Russell, why would it be important for you to find

out if Joseph Smith was called to be a prophet?"

This question is good for a variety of reasons, mainly because it helps the investigator to figure out for himself why he needs to know if what he has just heard is true. As you will find is true in life, most people like to figure out things for themselves. They do not want to be taught or told, they want to feel as if they have acquired their beliefs and conclusions on their own. It's the human way.

In truth, I am the same way, although I have worked hard over the years to develop my ability to learn as much as possible from the counsel of others. We are all a little stubborn, so as a missionary you must always help your investigators to teach themselves the gospel. All that is needed is your guidance. Please take heart to this advice.

Another reason why the previous question is so effective is because it helps to lead the investigator into the next topic of discussion, which is the Book of Mormon. If the investigator has stated that it would be important to find out that Joseph Smith really was a prophet, then he is going to need a way to come to such a conclusion. Of course, the Book of Mormon is the following link in the ongoing chain of the first discussion.

Principle Five: The Book of Mormon

By this point, the investigator should have expressed his desire to know if Joseph Smith was called to be a prophet to re-establish the Lord's church in these latter-days. (If he does not want to know, then it is a waste of time to continue with the discussion.) Since the Book of Mormon is his ticket to find out such an important fact, it is imperative that the facts of the Book of Mormon are explained clearly and logically to the investigator.

You would not believe how many times I heard this statement in my mission:

"Yes, I have talked with the missionaries and I think that book of yours speaks the truth, but I'll never leave my church."

Whenever I heard such a statement, I always wanted to slap myself on the forehead and scream at the top of my lungs, "No? You don't get it, do you? If you have heard the missionaries before and if you do believe in the Book of Mormon, you would never say such a contradictory statement!" Of course I never did come out and say anything like that, mainly because all that I could do in such a situation was re-teach the person the first discussion and stress the magnitude of the truth of the Book of Mormon more effectively.

Most people, even after hearing the first discussion, do not grasp the utter magnitude and importance of the Book of Mormon. They do not understand that if the book is true, then the Church is true. Somehow, when they were taught before by missionaries, they did not grasp how the Book of Mormon links us to Joseph Smith and helps us have no doubt that the message that we share as missionaries is true. In most cases, simply teaching Principle Five well can prevent this.

Here are a few of my suggestions for this important principle:

All copies of the Book of Mormon have illustrations at the beginning which go along with Principle Five. Use them in your teaching! Otherwise, when your investigator sees those pictures, he will have no clue whatsoever as to what they represent. I speak from my own experiences as an investigator on this one.

When explaining that Lehi came to America with his family, it is very helpful to have a map to show the difference between Jerusalem and Central America. This may not be very necessary in some missions, but many people in my mission had very little grasp on geography, and so if they heard that Lehi came over with his family, they had no idea that it meant that he had to cross an ocean. A simple map glued to your flipcharts can clear up many misconceptions that your investigators may have, as well as hold their interest better.

When explaining that Christ came to America, I have found that it is very helpful to also point out that while He (Jesus) was in America, he formed His church and taught many truths so that we would not confuse His doctrine. Continue by explaining how He taught the people the correct form of baptism, the name of His church, and important prayers. These statements will help the investigator to understand why the Lord decided that having only the Bible would not be sufficient. Almost all of your investigators, if they are Christian, will agree that all of the different doctrines of the many religious denominations are not what Christ had intended when he formed his church. The Book of Mormon is their answer to the confusion that currently exists in the world today.

Finish Principle Five with a powerful testimony. Put every bit of excitement and spirit you have into expressing your belief that Christ gave us the Book of Mormon so that we could leave the confusion that exists in the world today by knowing that the Church of Jesus Christ of Latter-day Saints is the Savior's church.

To finish the principle, a very effective question that will help you greatly is:

Why would it be important for you to know that the Book of Mormon is true?

Again, this helps solidify the link and move you into the following principle, which will tell the investigator how he can now find out if the Book of Mormon is true. Often, the investigator will say that if he knows that the Book of Mormon is true, then that affirms his belief in Christ. This is very true, but you need to help the investigator to also understand that if the Book of Mormon is true, then your whole message is true, which means that the Church of Jesus Christ of Latter-day Saints is the only true church on the face of the earth. It can be a little difficult for the investigator to comprehend such a bold statement, but with the help of Principle Six, you can make such a task possible. What magnitude Principle Five carries!

Principle Six: The Holy Ghost

To close your first discussion, you really need to finish with a "bang." The spiritual level at this point, as well as your challenges to the investigators to read and pray, is of utmost significance and importance. Here are a few pointers:

When explaining third Nephi eleven, be sure that you give a short synopsis of what the reader can expect. So many investigators, after having read the first few lines of third Nephi eleven, quit just because they are a little confused and do not understand the story line well. Also, when giving this synopsis, point out that Christ taught the proper way of baptism to the people in this chapter. This is very important because this reading is the link that prepares the investigator for the second discussion.

Read, *Ponder*, and *Pray*. Those three words mean so much to me. I can remember well that at the end of my first discussion with the elders, they challenged me to read, ponder, and pray more than once. Also, they mentioned the letters, RPP, which of course represent Read, Ponder, and Pray. As a missionary, you must do your best to imbed RPP in the mindset of your investigators. It is a great idea to repeat these three letters many times during the sixth principle because that way the investigator will easily remember his assignment which will lead him to the truth. Repetition, as you will quickly learn, is one of the best and most effective teaching tools that you will ever have. You cannot talk about nor explain the Book of Mormon promise enough times to your investigators. In fact, upon receiving the first discussion, your investigators should be able to teach to their own friends what they would have to do in order to find out if the Book of Mormon is true. If they cannot do this, then they certainly won't be able to do it on their own.

As a missionary, you have two methods that you can choose from to explain the Book of Mormon promise. Naturally, the first method that you may try is Moroni 10:3-5. I used these verses often in my mission, but I found that they were somewhat complex for many of my investigators. I also found that these verses were just what some of my investigators needed to search for the truth about our message as missionaries. As my mission continued, I started to use the last two paragraphs of the Introduction in the Book of Mormon more often to explain to my investigators the "Moroni promise." These two paragraphs are awesome and truly inspired, and they also reiterate some key points of the first discussion.

The next to last paragraph of the Introduction gives an easy-to-understand method in which the investigator can find out if the Book of Mormon is true. After you have made sure that the investigator completely understands what he has to do in order to find out the truth, you can then finish your discussion with the perfect "exclamation point," which will come in the last paragraph.

The final paragraph of the Introduction emphasizes what the investigator will *also* know if he finds out that the Book of Mormon is true. This paragraph clearly states that the investigator will gain *three more* profound truths: The first is that Jesus Christ is the Savior of the World; the second, that Joseph Smith was called to be a prophet (a true book could not be translated by a false prophet), and the third profound truth is that The Church of Jesus Christ of Latter-day Saints is the

Lord's kingdom (His Church) once again established on the earth. I love realizing what great knowledge can be gained just by having a simple testimony of the Book of Mormon! Your investigators should also feel such excitement and therefore have a burning need to know the truth and do their part to find such truth for themselves. I would suggest that after you have committed your investigators to read, ponder, and pray about the truthfulness of the Book of Mormon, that you also ask this question, which will greatly help you to get a feel for just how much your investigator has understood the depth and magnitude of your lesson:

"What will you do if you learn that the Book of Mormon is true?"

Yes, it is quite a bold question, but it will help the investigator to progress and to really search for the truth. Answers will vary when this question is asked, but at times you will hear, "Well, I guess I will have to consider that your message, as well as your church, is true." Whenever you hear such an answer, you must praise and encourage the investigator more than ever before. Such a response should be music to a missionary's ears. It is the concept that you have spent forty five minutes trying to help the investigator understand. During this time period you have done nothing but help your investigator to comprehend the magnitude of your message. It pains me deeply when investigators listen to the first discussion without at all grasping its significance, and how important it is in their lives.

Finally, the discussion has just about come to an end. You now should have made a return appointment (get back to their house as soon as possible, otherwise Satan will have more of a chance to produce doubts in their minds) and the investigators should know that when you return to their house you will want to know how it went with their RPP. To finish the discussion, it is always necessary to end with a prayer. At this point, it is good to show the steps of the prayer in the first discussion pamphlet and also give an "example" prayer to the investigator so that he knows more or less what to say when he says his own prayer. (Again, whether you do this depends on your investigator) If you just mention the steps to your investigator but do not give any clearer explanation, you have probably accomplished very little. A sample prayer can vary, but the main point is that you stress that the investigator must ask specific questions in order to receive specific answers. So many people never find out that the Book of Mormon is true simply because they never ask their Father in Heaven for an answer. Do not let this happen! Make sure that every investigator that you ever have the pleasure of teaching understands clearly just what he must do and say to know the truth, and also what he will feel. I'll give you an example:

"Mr. Venezuela, I have just shown you and your family the steps of prayer, and now I would like to give you an example as to what you might say in your prayer after you have read and pondered third Nephi, eleven. Dear Heavenly Father: I am grateful for having read this book. I have pondered what it teaches about Christ coming to America and also about baptism. I feel that it might be true. How do You feel about that?"

Notice that I have not used an example that finishes with a yes or no question. I am not saying that there is anything wrong with yes or no questions addressed to Heavenly Father, but I personally feel that as children of our Father in Heaven, we must present Him with our feelings about a subject and then see if these feelings meet His approval. This method of prayer can be applied to so many other things, but in all cases it is very effective when said in faith. Whether you as a missionary use this method or not, the main objective is still the same, your investigators must clearly know what they must do in order to be blessed with an answer about the truthfulness of your message and the Book of Mormon.

If you properly expound on what the investigator is to do (RPP) before your return visit, then when that visit rolls around, you should not hear the excuse "Well, I read but I forgot to pray." We know that after such a clearly taught first discussion, the investigator would not honestly say such a statement and mean it. This is because they have had RPP repeated to them five times already. I promise you that if you teach Principle Six well and the investigator says that they forgot to pray after having read third Nephi eleven, then the real reason was not because they forgot, but rather because they were afraid to pray or that they just elected not to. You must find out what this reason is whenever you find that your investigators have not prayed before your second visit.

Make sure that you express to your investigators just how sure you are that they are going to do their part to find out the truth about the Book of Mormon. Instill in them your confidence and enthusiasm. You will see that many times your investigators will read just so they can see how enthusiastically you will react after they have told you that they did their RPP.

After having taught the first discussion, you should already have formed a strong bond with your investigators. The spirit of the message, as well as your enthusiasm, has formed a strong link. This relationship should grow throughout the six discussions and beyond.

Let us review the "chain" and "links" of the first discussion.

Eternal happiness is made possible through the teachings of Jesus Christ, which are made known to us through prophets and the Holy Ghost. Joseph Smith is one of these prophets, and was called in these latter days to lead us out of confusion. We can know that Joseph Smith was called of God upon reading the Book of Mormon and then following the promptings of the Holy Ghost.

Remember, the success of each link is contingent on how well the investigator understands the previous links.

Chapter Eleven:

The Second Discussion

I'm completely fired up to analyze the second discussion. When you talk to your fellow missionaries, you will hear people say that they have certain discussions that are their favorites. Well, I have my favorite, and I hope that after reading this chapter, you will have chosen your favorite as well. The second discussion provides you with the opportunity to really exercise your power as a messenger of Christ. I cannot emphasize enough the importance of constantly practicing the second discussion to the point that you become a master at its principles and also the possible scenarios that go along with helping your investigators make the commitments of this discussion.

Upon starting the second discussion, like always, it is requisite that you find out if your investigators have done their part and read and prayed since your last visit. If such has not occurred, and they have yet to do their RPP's, I would suggest not teaching the second discussion until they have followed through with their commitments. If you do teach the second discussion despite the lack of effort on the investigator's part, ninety nine percent of the time you will find that they will not be prepared to open up to your teachings and accept the baptismal invitation. Of course, if you do feel prompted by the Spirit, you have the option to teach the second discussion. During my mission, I taught the second discussion many times even though the investigators had not prayed, but I would only do this after having learned that they had at least read and felt that what they read was true. As you progress in your mission, you will gain the experience needed to know when to continue with the discussions or instead resolve doubts and review previously taught doctrine.

I have also found that people are more inclined to commit to baptism if they have already attended church. Do your best to bring your investigators to church at least one time before they receive any type of baptismal invitation. This will help them to feel much more comfortable with any commitments that they may make.

I would like to introduce to you in this chapter many of the techniques and methods that I used to make this discussion as successful as possible. I can earnestly say that I, as well as many other missionaries in my mission, used these same methods and found them to be very successful. I would ask that you would do the same and open up your heart to my suggestions and give them a try. I would imagine that much of the information taught in this chapter is already used in your mission area, which is incentive for you to experiment with these teaching techniques.

Principles One and Two: The Atonement

The second discussion consists mainly of two distinct parts: The first part is made up of principles One and Two, which break down the Atonement, describing the physical death as well as the spiritual death. Although a strong testimony of the Atonement of our Savior is very critical as a member of the Church of Jesus Christ of Latter-day Saints, it is not very pertinent that your investigators fully understand what the Atonement is before they are baptized. I have been a member now for over five years and I feel that I am a long way from grasping the magnitude and full understanding of the Atonement. Also, since the Atonement is a rather complicated subject, your investigators will often not grasp the basics of its teachings as they begin to receive the discussions. (I speak from my own experience.) This is okay. That is why we have church on Sundays, so that all of us can slowly understand more and more about the Atonement as well as the rest of the plan of salvation. My point is that you do not need to spend too much time on the first two principles of the second discussion.

One of the most common visual aids used by missionaries in the second discussion uses pictures of a car, mud puddles, and bridges (or something similar) to describe the two obstacles that we must overcome in this life (sin and death). I don't want to discount this visual aid, but I feel that it should be used in a separate visit, mainly because it takes too long and is not needed if the missionary teaches the principle clearly.

The amount of time that you spend on the first two principles of the second discussion should be minimal, mainly so that they do not take away from the time that you have to spend talking about baptism. Teach what the first two principles say and that should be sufficient. I would also recommend some sort of simple demonstration to explain how the spirit separates from the body and then reunites with the body after the resurrection. The well-known glove(body)-and-hand(spirit) example is quite sufficient. If you teach clearly and ask good questions, your investigators will have at least a decent understanding of the basics of the Atonement. Like always, you can test this understanding by asking "find out" questions at the end of the principle.

Principle Three: Faith

Principle Three introduces the second half of the second discussion. Although this is not a very time-consuming principle, I believe it is of great importance in order to help the investigator to commit to baptism.

The main focus of this principle is on the fact that there are two—not just one—parts of faith. Faith requires a belief and also an action, the latter being the most important aspect. So many of your investigators will feel that the simple act of believing in God and his son Jesus Christ will lead them to eternal happiness. You must help them realize that this is not the case. Too often, missionaries do not stress this enough. Scriptures can be helpful, but I have found that questions that help the investigator to contemplate what faith really is are usually the most effective ways to reach a consensus with the investigator. Such questions could include:

"Why would it be important that we show our faith through our actions?" or " Why would it be necessary to have works and actions, and not just a belief, in order to live with Heavenly Father after this life?"

These questions are very basic, but they will help your investigators to really analyze why they must "act" in order to reach eternal happiness. Simply asking the investigator what they feel about faith is usually not enough. Once the investigator understands the concept of what faith really is, including its two parts, you can move on to the fourth principle. Faith is the first of a series of critical "links" that will lead you to the baptismal challenge, which is the climax of the discussion.

Principle Four: Repentance

By this point, you are about halfway through the second discussion. You need to do your best to ensure that there is quite a high level of energy and excitement with each principle that you teach with this discussion. Do all that you can to raise the level of spirituality and excitement with each new principle. By the time you make the baptismal challenge, the spiritual level should be peaking. This will be discussed much more in depth at the end of this chapter.

Principle Four is pretty simple. Your goal is to ensure that the investigator has a clear understanding of what the steps of repentance are, as well as the fact that we must repent before and after baptism. Again, asking a question about to the steps of repentance will help you to know if the investigator understands what repentance is.

Principles Five, Six, and Seven (in certain languages): Baptism and the Holy Ghost

I only want to give three tips for the final three principles. Here they are:

—Be bold with regard to everything you teach.

—If doubts arise about The Church of Jesus Christ of Latter-day Saints being the only church with the Lord's authority to baptize, explain to your investigator that you will go much more in depth on the subject in the third discussion.

—Testify with power! Put every ounce of strength you have into showing your investigators what baptism means to you.

Basically, principles five, six, and seven relay to the investigator why they should be baptized into the Lord's church. Then, after you have taught the principles and before you have offered any type of baptismal invitation, I would strongly suggest that you ask what I call the "golden question," which is:

"From what you have learned today, why is it important

that you are baptized in the Church of Jesus Christ of Latter-day Saints?"

This is a very bold, but very effective question. It will help your investigators begin to think about baptism on their own, and therefore realize the importance of getting baptized into the Lord's church. My investigators would often answer this question by stating that they would be able to live with God after death. I would then give them some positive feedback and tell them that they have the opportunity to be baptized in the Church of Jesus Christ of Latter-day Saints, but first they have to do certain things so that they could know for certain that the church was true and that they were committed to being a life-long member. Here is an example:

Elder: "Baptism in the Church of Jesus Christ of Latter-day Saints does help enable us to return to live with Heavenly Father. Mr. Taylor, you have the opportunity to be baptized in the Lord's church. As missionaries, we teach six discussions which help people to understand the doctrine of church. In order for you to be baptized, you will have to participate in these six discussions and also attend church at least two times. (This number can vary depending on the mission.) You would also need to read, ponder, and pray during the six discussions to help you know with a surety that you want to take this important step in your life. Therefore, Mr. Taylor, if you do these things that we have mentioned, and desire to be baptized after having received the discussions and attended church the appropriate number of times, you can be baptized in the Lord's church on the sixteenth (or whatever date is suggested) of this month. How do you feel about this?"

Notice what I have done here. Not once have I asked the investigator to be baptized. Rather then just dropping a bomb on him out of the blue, I have told him what one must do in order to be baptized. This will help him to continue to feel the

Spirit and contemplate the things that I have told him. His answer is likely to be something like this:

"Well, elder, to tell you the truth, I am not ready to be baptized into another church" or "That seems a little soon, don't you think?"

I would always expect to hear this type of statement. In fact, it is the same thing that I told the elders when they invited me to be baptized. The key is in your response.

Elder: "Mr. Taylor, we understand that you are not yet ready to be baptized. That is why we teach the six discussions and have you attend church first. After doing these things as well as your RPP, you can be sure of your decision. But then again, Mr. Taylor, if you receive the discussions and go to church and do your part to find out if you want to take this important step in your life, you still have the option of not getting baptized. It is all up to you. Only you can make the decision."

Mr. Taylor: "I see what you boys are telling me. What you are saying is that if I feel that your message and Church are true after I do these things, and I then want to be baptized on the sixteenth, then I can be baptized."

Elder: "That is exactly right. Let's look at it this way: Let's say you do everything we discussed and the sixteenth rolls around and you decide not to be baptized. What happens then?

Mr. Taylor: "Well, then I guess I don't get baptized."

Elder: "Exactly. It seems like you understand well. Therefore, Mr. Taylor, if you do your part and feel that the Church and our message is true when the sixteenth rolls around, then what will you do?"

Mr. Taylor: "If I feel it is true, then I will get baptized."

Elder: "Great! We have the utmost faith that you will receive your answer. We congratulate you on your demonstration of faith and your desire to follow the Savior's example. We promise to do our part and prepare you. The rest of it will be up to you."

Well, there it is. I feel that this is one of the best ways to give a baptismal invitation. In this method, the investigator is the one who actually does a self-challenge baptismal by saying that he will get baptized if he feels the message is true. To help you to understand this further, let me use my best friend as an example. He is of another faith and I have asked him before if he would join the church if he found out for himself that it was true. He has said yes, but the hard part is getting him to do his part so that he can find out his answer. Any fool would see the logic in getting baptized into the Lord's true Church, it is just that most people will not commit to and follow through with baptismal preparation. Therefore, the key to conversion is not so much baptismal invitations as it is the idea of one agreeing to—and then doing—all that they can to know if the Church of Jesus Christ of Latter-day Saints is true. Once you have accomplished this as a missionary, you are in great shape.

As I stated earlier, you want the spiritual level of the second discussion to gradually climb, peaking at your baptismal invitation. So many people get "turned off" in the second discussion because they are not prepared to receive the baptismal challenge, mainly because they have not been well-prepared by the missionaries to receive such an invitation. They often feel that if they say, "Yes," then there is no turning back, and therefore they end up saying, "No," and the progress of the investigator then stops. Do not let this happen! By doing the baptismal challenge in the manner that we have discussed, you are helping the investigator to feel in charge and in control of his own destiny. You are showing him that only he can make this important decision. When it comes down to it, you are giving your investigators a sense of empowerment, and that is something that every man and woman desires to have. No one wants to be told what to do. People want to feel like every decision that they make in life is one that they have made for themselves. This is absolutely true with regards to the discussions. I testify that this is an amazing truth and it can drastically change the course of your mission.

I hope that you have followed me up to this point. Please experiment with this method and you will see great results, just as many missionaries in the past have seen. Notice also that at the end of the discussion, I reiterated the baptismal date. This is crucial. Your investigators must have a baptismal goal date. Without such a date, there will be inevitable complacency and your investigators will not feel a sense of urgency to find out if what they are hearing is true. Never leave the second discussion without a baptismal goal date! If you do, you basically have wasted about an hour.

I can remember well the second discussion in which the elders and I set my baptismal goal date. I blatantly told them that I did not think that I would be ready and that I really did not think I wanted to join their church. But—and I want to stress this part—I did promise to them (after I felt a sense of empowerment) that I would do my part to know if their message was true. Needless to say, I did my part and was baptized on November 8, 1994, the exact date that I set with the elders during the second discussion. They were great missionaries. They helped me to feel relaxed and in charge. They enabled me to commit myself to doing my part, which in turn was what brought about my conversion.

Before closing this chapter, I want to make one last point: Even though a baptismal goal date is a must for your investigators at the end of the second discussion, you still have the responsibility as a missionary to only let your investigators be baptized when you know that they are committed to, and are living, the gospel of Jesus Christ. Never fall into the trap of letting someone be baptized who is not fully committed to living the rest of his life by the standards of the Church of Jesus Christ of Latter-day Saints. If you ever have an investigator reach his baptismal goal date with the desire to be baptized but not the actions to merit such a step (example: Word of wisdom problems), it is your duty to postpone the baptism until the investigator is living the gospel. The Church does not need numbers, it needs converts. We are builders of the Kingdom, and true conversion is our only means of achieving such a goal.

The hints and techniques in this chapter work. I know of this with a surety. If you implement them in your teachings as a missionary, you will soon be saying, as well as teaching to others, the same thing.

Now do yourself a favor and go back and read this whole chapter again, and then go on to Chapter Twelve.

Chapter Twelve:

The Frank Discussion

This is one of the most important chapters that you will read in this whole book. You may not fully understand why this is so right now, but you will certainly find out as time goes by in your mission. I feel that the three most important discussions that missionaries teach are the First Discussion, the Second Discussion, and the "Frank Discussion." I suppose that most people reading this book would be surprised to read the Frank Discussion in this list, but I will tell you why this is so.

I cannot tell you how many times I would talk to people in my mission who had previously investigated the church and had stopped meeting with the missionaries without knowing exactly why the missionaries stopped coming over and teaching them. This should never happen! If you decide to stop teaching your investigators for whatever reason (usually because they are not doing their part to know if the church is true), then you must explain to them why you have decided to make such a decision. As you become a master at teaching the "Frank Discussion," your investigators will always know why you have decided to stop teaching them the gospel.

As missionaries, we tend to spend so much time teaching non-progressing investigators that we end up wasting most of our "find" time because we are working with people who just aren't doing their part to know if the message is true. It is critical, as I have stated previously, that you do not waste a moment of your time as a missionary. There is nothing worse than spending months teaching a family only to have them reject your message in the end because they have been lackadaisical in searching for the truth. This happens all of the time, and it usually happens because the investigators just don't comprehend your position as a missionary and what the magnitude of the message is that you are sharing. Your job is to ensure that all of your investigators feel the need to take your message seriously so that they can be converted through their own efforts of reading, pondering, praying, church attendance, and so on.

It is a must that you realize your power and authority as a missionary, as well as the importance and need to help convert or leave your investigators as soon as possible. Although conversion is not an easy process, and although it can be very time consuming, you can speed up the process of conversion in each person you reach while out in the mission field. The Frank Discussion is often the key that you will need to unlock the doors of conversion and to jump-start the spiritual engines of your investigators.

Samuel the Lamanite: The master of the Frank Discussion. To really understand what the Frank Discussion is, as well as the steps to its effectiveness, we must analyze what Samuel the Lamanite said to the Nephites just before the time of the Savior's birth. Samuel, in chapters 13-16 of Helaman, gives us the perfect example of how to perform a Frank Discussion. Let us analyze his steps:

In Helaman 13:2-3, we learn that Samuel had attempted to preach to the wicked Nephites who were in the land of Zarahemla. These Nephites rejected his message and even cast him out of their city. Samuel then left Zarahemla, but was prompted by the Lord to return to the Nephites to do one last thing.

What do you think this "one last thing" was that Samuel was commanded to do?

Well, if you guessed that he was sent back in order to give

a frank discussion to the Nephites, you guessed right. Therefore, in verses five and six, Samuel returns to the Nephites and
begins to preach to them. Notice from reading these verses,
that Samuel does not start off saying that his message comes
from his mouth, but from the words that the Lord "doth put
into my heart." Your investigators must also realize that the
message that you share is not something that you made up, but
rather the Lord's Plan of Happiness. This is the only way to get
the attention and respect of the people you teach.

Samuel continues to bear testimony and reiterate that
the message he shares is not just any message. He states, "an
angel of the Lord hath declared it unto me, and he did bring
glad tidings to my soul. And behold, I was sent unto you to
declare it unto you also, that ye might have glad tidings; but
behold ye would not receive me."

Ouch! Can you start to see why we call this a frank
discussion? It consists of the bold, blunt truth. Samuel declares
unto the Nephites that he was sent unto them to preach to
them the Plan of Salvation. You, too, are sent as a representative of Jesus Christ unto the world to preach his gospel. Don't
be afraid to admit that! Your investigators must realize that it
is not a coincidence that you are at their houses teaching them
the gospel. They must know that the Lord has sent you there.
Also, just as Samuel told the Nephites that they had not done
their part (rejected him), you must relay the same information
to the people you teach. If they are not doing their part to know
the truth, tell them (in a loving way)!

We have now read a few of the initial steps of a frank
discussion, but if we continue to analyze Samuel's speech, we
can learn much more. In Helaman 14:30-31, Samuel states:
"and now remember, remember, my brethren, that whosoever
perisheth, perisheth unto himself; and whosoever doeth iniq-
uity, doeth it unto himself; for behold, ye are free; ye are

permitted to act for yourselves; for behold, God hath given unto you a knowledge and he hath made you free.

"He hath given unto you that ye might know good from evil, and he hath given unto you that ye might choose life or death..."

What topic is Samuel explaining to the Nephites in this portion of his talk?

If you guessed free agency, you are correct. He is telling the Nephites that they must choose for themselves to follow the Lord and his plan. You, too, must help your investigators to see that they are the only ones who can find out the truth. You can bear your testimony all day and all night, but if an investigator is not willing to open his heart and seek the truth, your testimony is in vain. Samuel pointed out to the Nephites that the message that he was sharing was a life-and-death matter, and so it should be treated as such. Your investigators must also understand this.

Moving on with Samuel's frank discussion, in chapter 15:3 he talks about the love the Lord has for the Nephites. Love is such a major factor in the success that a missionary has, and that is why your investigators need to feel that you, as well as the Lord, love them. In fact, the love that you truly have for your investigators will be the most important factor of just how successful your frank discussions are.

Finally, by the time we reach Helaman 16, Samuel has finished his frank discussion, and now we can see what were the results of his labor in the first verse of the chapter.

"And now it came to pass that there were many who heard the words of Samuel the Lamanite which he spake upon the walls of the city. And as many as believed on his word went forth and sought for Nephi; and when they had come forth and found him they confessed unto him their sins and denied not, desiring that they might be baptized unto the Lord."

Wow! Is this an awesome verse or what? Can you see the result of Samuel's frank discussion with the Nephites? What would have happened if he had not listened to the Lord and gone back to teach a frank discussion? Obviously, all of the Nephites would have perished. But, because of Samuel's diligence, many Nephites were saved.

You, too, will find yourself in Samuel's position many times in your mission. So often, you will see that your investigators are not progressing because they are not doing their parts. When you have this feeling, it is time to teach the frank discussion. Not doing so could mean grave results.

The steps of the Frank Discussion. I am sure that by now you realize just how significant the Frank Discussion is with regards to the salvation of many of Heavenly Father's children. Following here are the steps for teaching the Frank Discussion. These steps, just like the rest of the suggestions in this book, are meant to be experimented with. They are not cut and dried by any means, although I feel that each aspect of the discussion needs to be addressed when the time comes to teach your investigators. Here are the steps:

—Find out if the investigator has fulfilled his commitment or promise.
—Find out why the investigator has not fulfilled his commitment if necessary.
—Find out if the message that you are sharing is important to the investigator.

This can be accomplished by asking a few questions. For example:

"Would it be important for you, Mr. Lopez, to find out if the message that we are sharing with you is true? Why?"

"In what ways can the Church of Jesus Christ of Latter-day Saints change your life?"

The missionary should share with the investigator how he feels about the investigator not completing his part.

The missionary should share his purpose or calling, the power of this calling, and the fact that there are many persons waiting to hear the gospel at this time.

The missionary should share his love for the investigator and his desire that the investigator progresses and can live with Heavenly Father, emphasize the fact that all of the progress depends on the investigator and find out if the investigator is ready to do his part to know the truth. For example, if he will:

—*Read, Ponder, Pray*
—*Attend church*
—*Obey the Word of Wisdom*
—*Pray specifically to find out if he should be baptized*

If the investigator is ready to do his or her part, you must congratulate him and get him pumped up for the commitment that he has just made. If the investigator says that he is not willing to do his part to learn the truth, the missionary should thank him for his honesty and move on.

Looking at these steps, you might think that it would be very difficult to become good at teaching the Frank Discussion. I would be lying to you if I said that it is easy, but through hard work and practice, it can be mastered. Here is an example of a common frank discussion that I often dealt with in my mission. This example takes place after the missionaries have taught the first discussion to an investigator. They have since read with the investigator, who had not done his *Read, Ponder,* and *Pray* after the first discussion. Upon meeting with the investigator this third time, the missionaries have much faith that the investigator will have at least read some of the Book of Mormon.

Missionaries: "Mr. Lopez, we are excited to be here with you today and find out how your reading went. So, how did it go?"

Mr. Lopez: "Well boys, to be honest with you, with my busy work schedule, I still have not been able to read."

Missionary: "Oh, well we are sorry to hear that you have not had time to read and pray. Is there any other reason that you have not mentioned to us as to why you have yet to read and pray about the message that we have shared with you?"

Mr. Lopez: "Nope, I just have not had the time."

Missionary: "Mr. Lopez, we are going to be very honest with you right now, and we want you to be very honest with us. Agreed?"

Mr. Lopez: "I can do that."

Missionary: "Great. Mr. Lopez, would it really be important for you to find out if the message that we are sharing is true?"

Mr. Lopez: "Well, I think that it would be, but I just have a lot going on in my life right now."

Missionary: "Why would it be important that you find out if our message is true?"

Mr. Lopez: "Well, I guess if there is a "true" church out there like you boys say there is, then I should know about it."

Missionary: "Exactly! But why else would it be important?"

Mr. Lopez: "Well, you all talk about how this church focuses on the family, and I could really use some help with my teenagers."

Missionary: "Nice point. As you can see, Mr. Lopez, there are various reasons as to why you must find out if this message is true. This is why it hurts us to see that you have yet to do your part and Read, Ponder, and Pray as we have already talked about quite a few times. Mr. Lopez, you must understand that we truly are representatives of the Lord Jesus Christ. He has sent us both here to teach you and your family the gospel. This is all that we do. We teach people who are willing to open up their hearts and search for the truth. Our success does not really depend on our actions as much as it depends on the people that we teach.

"We can preach and teach all day, but this does not matter unless one wants to find the truth for himself. We care about you, Mr. Lopez. We have enjoyed the feelings that we have had in your home since we began to teach you and your family. We desire that you, as well as the rest of your family, can experience eternal happiness, living with our Father in Heaven. But again, I would remind you that only you have the power to make such happiness a reality."

Second Missionary: "That's right, Mr. Lopez. You have a very special family with much potential. But like my companion said, on whom does your progress depend?"

Mr. Lopez: "I can see that it depends on me."

Missionary: "Yes, and therefore, what would you have to do in order to know that our message is true?"

Mr. Lopez: "I would have to read, ponder, and pray."

Missionary: "Exactly. Therefore, Mr. Lopez, are you now willing and ready to read from the parts that we have marked for you in the Book of Mormon, ponder it, and ask our Heavenly Father in humble and earnest prayer if it is true?"

Mr. Lopez: "Yes I am. I am going to do it."

Missionary: "Great! We have the utmost faith that you will receive an answer when you do these things. We would like to come over again on Thursday and see how everything went. Can you have this done by Thursday?"

Mr. Lopez: "I can."

Missionary: "Wonderful! Then we will see you Thursday. But I must tell you now, Mr. Lopez, if you elect not to do your part this time, we will probably have to move on so that we can work with the many other people that are searching for the truth. I would like to thank you for being sincere with us today. I feel that we have gotten a lot of things worked out. We will be praying for you throughout the week."

I hope you now have a good idea of how to do a frank discussion. It takes faith and boldness, but it is your best means of motivating, or moving on with, your investigators. The Frank Discussion can be used in many situations. I have listed a few of them:

—When the investigator has repeatedly not read or prayed.
—When the investigator promises that he will go to church and doesn't.
—When an investigator does not do his part to prepare for baptism.

These are just a few of the possible cases which you will have to deal with, the most common for all missionaries being the first. I have listed a few more tips to help you with the frank discussion:

—Your investigators will often say that they have not had the time to read and pray. I will be blunt in saying that this is false ninety nine percent of the time. Most people just don't make the effort to read, ponder and pray. They do not feel that knowing whether the message is true or not is that important. Simply put, they do not understand the magnitude of what they are dealing with, which is eternal happiness. The Frank Discussion will help them to realize this better and hopefully they will then start to take you, as well as your message, more seriously. Everyone has the time to read, ponder, and pray! It is all about priorities.

—When you begin the Frank Discussion, it is very important to always emphasize the need to be honest with each other.

—Give frank discussions often. Before dropping any of your investigators you should do your best to give them a frank discussion. This way no one will ever be left wondering why you stopped coming over to teach them.

—The Spirit must be present in the frank discussion. This is made possible only through the love you have for the people you teach. The Frank Discussion should never be used as an opportunity to flex your muscles as a missionary. If your investigator decides that he or she is not ready to search for the truth, then they should leave the experience with a respect for the missionaries, not anger towards them.

—Be sincerely enthusiastic.

—Radiate your love.

—When taught and used properly, the Frank Discussion can save the souls of many persons. All we have to do is ponder the example that Samuel gave us and we can see for ourselves that the Frank Discussion is just as important as any of the discussions in the discussion booklet. I saw many people enter into the waters of baptism in   my mission only after they decided to really try and do their part to see if the message was true. Such an effort was spawned by the Frank Discussion. Although not everyone is saved, at least many do change their hearts and turn their thoughts to Heavenly Father and his plan.

Chapter Thirteen

The Great 3 Nephi 11

If there is one complete chapter that you have a chance of memorizing while on your mission without even trying it would be the chapter of, 3 Nephi 11, which is the first reading assignment given to investigators after the first discussion. I cannot stress enough the importance and magnitude of this wonderful and enlightening portion of the Book of Mormon. Because you will be reading and using this chapter so much with your investigators, it is absolutely necessary that you have a firm grasp and understanding of what this chapter teaches us as well as the potential effect that it can have on your investigators. This is why I have written this chapter of the book.

3 Nephi 11 can and will work miracles in your mission. That is its purpose. That is why Mormon put it in the Book of Mormon and abridged it as he did. That is also why the brethren of the Church decided to make it a focal point of the discussions and a link between the first and second discussions. As you read the following paragraphs, you will likely see a part of 3 Nephi 11 that you may have never seen before. I feel that it is the part that Mormon wanted you, me, and everyone else in these latter days to see.

History. To begin to understand 3 Nephi 11, we must first look at who wrote the chapter. It was originally written by Nephi (#3), who was the son of Nephi (#2), who was the son of Helaman, who was the son of Alma the younger, who was the son of Alma. Are you still with me? Well, I know that this family tree can get a little confusing, but if you are at all familiar with

Nephi's ancestors, you can see that it is an ancestry loaded with some of the greatest missionaries of all time.

I would imagine that Nephi (#3) had many talks with his father regarding missionary work. Think about this: Nephi (#2), along with his brother, Lehi, were two of the most successful missionaries ever. At one point during their ministry, they baptized eight thousand souls! Isn't that mind boggling? Nephi had the ability given to him by Heavenly Father to invoke the powers of Heaven and thereby had power to do whatever he desired. (See Helaman 10:6-7.) To make a long story short, Nephi (#2) was as good as they come in regards to bringing souls to Christ. What do you think that Nephi and his son talked about at the dinner table? You can rest assured that Nephi was taught a few things about converting people unto the Savior and his gospel. I honestly believe that Nephi (#3) took much of the advice given to him by his father and used it when he wrote the full portion of 3 Nephi 11.

We also must take a quick look at the other great man that was responsible for giving us 3 Nephi 11—Mormon. Mormon, who was responsible for abridging the Book of Mormon, was also responsible for abridging 3 Nephi. He only had the time and the space to include in the plates the most important information of what happened when Christ visited the Nephites. I believe that when Mormon abridged this chapter (3 Nephi 11), he had at least two purposes in mind: One, he wanted to give a general account of the Savior's visit to the American people. And two, because Mormon could see the mass confusion that we would have in these latter days, he would therefore want to clear up much of the false doctrine that was to be taught among the many religions of our time period. Mormon certainly accomplished his goals, and now we will start to analyze how he managed to achieve such a task.

The Savior taught some very important doctrines as soon as he appeared to the Nephites as we read in 3 Nephi 11. As you already know, the first subject that he instructed the Nephites on was Baptism. In his instructions, the Savior mentions the four requisites of a true baptism. Whenever I read this chapter with an investigator during my mission, I would make a point of emphasizing the verses that we are about to discuss. I hope that, from this general explanation, you will be able to help your investigators understand the power that is contained within this chapter. Also, when you start to read 3 Nephi 11 with an investigator, explain to him before starting that Christ, and not the missionary, will be the teacher of the discussion and that he will show the four requisites of a true baptism. Also, explain that the Savior will point out the reward of getting baptized in the manner he taught as well as what we will receive if we follow in his church until the end.

Requisite One. In verses 21 and 22, we read: "And the Lord said unto him: I give unto you power that ye shall baptize this people when I am again ascended into heaven. And again the Lord called others, and said unto them likewise; and he gave unto them power..."

This teaches your investigators the first requisite of the baptism of Jesus Christ, which is that of having an authority. In the fifth principle of the second discussion, we read: "Baptism must be performed by members of the Church who have the priesthood and are authorized to perform ordinances in the name of Christ." As you can see, 3 Nephi 11 and the second discussion both emphasize authority, but there are also other similarities that this chapter has with the second discussion that we will soon read. When reading these verses with an investigator, it is important to find out what the investigator feels about baptismal authority. This is also a good time for you to mention that The Church of Jesus Christ of Latter-day Saints is the only church with the Lord's authority to baptize.

Requisites Two and Three. In verse 23, we read: "Verily I say unto you, that whoso repenteth of his sins through your words, and desireth to be baptized in my name, on this wise shall ye baptize them..." Here, the Savior is teaching us that in order for one to be baptized he must have faith and be repentant (principles three and four of second discussion). It is very important that your investigators understand that the Savior taught this so that the people would understand the fact that baptism is a covenant requiring faith and repentance. To take this one step further, we also learn from these teachings that one must attain the *age of responsibility* to make such a covenant. Remember those three words! They are crucial in your success with members of other churches. Although most people in Chile are Catholic, I found that the majority of these people have questioned the practice of children being baptized as infants. If you explain to your investigators that Christ taught that faith and repentance were requisite for baptism, and therefore infants have no need to be baptized, they will therefore begin to see one of the many reasons that we have been given the Book of Mormon. Also, since there are so many people who feel that infant baptisms are wrong, agreeing with the Book of Mormon will help them start to form a bond with the work, which is very important in one's conversion as well as life in the church.

Requisite Four. The fourth requisite is found in verse 26, which states: "And then shall ye immerse them in the water, and come forth again out of the water."—Simple but to the point. We now have learned that the fourth requisite of the Savior's baptism is complete immersion in water. This also goes along with Principle Five in the second discussion. I found that reading this verse with investigators was helpful in having them realize, just through their own understanding of what was being taught by the Savior, that baptism by immersion is the only true way in which we can follow the example of Christ. In fact, many times in my mission, investigators would tell me that reading those verses helped them come to the knowledge that they had not received the Lord's proper baptism.

This brings me to a very important point: 3 Nephi 11 is such a great conversion tool because it shows everyone who reads it as to why all other churches are not true, none of them have *His* baptism. It is impressive that no names of other churches are even mentioned in the chapter. Yes, Nephi and Mormon were two wise missionaries. They understood the commitment pattern and they knew how to teach the true gospel without "bashing" others. This is also why we have been given 3 Nephi 11 and the rest of the Book of Mormon. Together with our testimonies, they are the greatest conversion tools that we have been empowered to use as a missionary. They speak the truth for themselves and when read under the proper conditions, this truth cannot be denied.

After reading with your investigators the four requisites of the Savior's baptism, the next step is for you to help them to understand the significance of verses 34 and 35. We read, "And whoso believeth in me, and is baptized, the same shall be saved; and they are they who shall inherit the kingdom of God. And whoso believeth not in me, and is not baptized, shall be damned."

As you can see, the Savior is very frank in telling us the truth about baptism and its benefits. He is very straight forward and therefore these verses are the "exclamation point" of 3 Nephi 11. After reading and discussing the four requisites with my investigators, as well as these two important verses, I would always ask this simple question: "From what the Savior has taught us today, what will we receive if we follow his example by getting baptized with the four requisites that he taught, and then follow in his path until the end?" (I always felt that it was important to mention following until the end so that the investigators would understand that there was much more to living with God than just getting baptized properly.)

The investigator would usually respond to the question by stating something to the effect that they could then live with Heavenly Father. After discussing the idea of inheriting the Kingdom of God, I would then ask one other question to see if the investigator had really understood what they had heard that day, which was: "What happens if one is not baptized in the manner the Savior taught and does not follow him until the end?"

Again, the answer would usually be related to what the Savior says in verse 35. At this point in the discussion, I would usually invite the investigators to baptism, but only if I felt that they had grasped and believed what they had heard during our review of 3 Nephi 11, as well as felt the Spirit.

To close this chapter, I would like to reiterate the fact that you must use 3 Nephi 11 often and wisely, and whenever you do read it with an investigator, make sure that the goal of your reading is to have them fully understand the Savior's doctrine on baptism; His four requisites as well as the reward of this act of faith. This knowledge can only be accomplished by asking many questions. A find-out question should be used following each requisite to understand if your investigator is following what the Savior is teaching.

Your investigators aren't assigned to read 3 Nephi 11 just because the brethren who wrote the discussion really liked the chapter. To the contrary, they understood that it could have a profound effect on all readers if it is understood and believed.

They also knew that it would prepare them for the second discussion. Make sure your investigators understand well the four requisites of the Lord's baptism. In fact, they should understand them so well that they should be able to teach their friends the four requisites of the Lord's baptism. Keep this in mind when you are teaching. You must be clear, concise, bold, and have the influence of the Spirit as you read this incredible chapter. If you do this, you will begin to see just what Nephi and Mormon had intended when they embarked on the Book of Mormon.

Chapter Fourteen:

Resolving Concerns
in the Book of Mormon

One of the greatest and most sought-after skills used in the mission field is that of resolving concerns. No matter where you go or whom you come in contact with in the mission field, you will always be confronted with doubts from the people that you teach. In order to be a great teacher, you must be able to resolve doubts, or at least alleviate them, at a second's notice. Here are my suggestions for doing so:

—Know the *commitment pattern*: The commitment pattern is not to be taken likely. Practice it daily. Once you have mastered it, you are in a position to resolve many concerns. The best missionaries that I have ever seen were masters of the commitment pattern.

—Learn to be a great listener: You may have read this suggestion from Steven Covey or Dale Carnegie, but every man and woman in this world wants to be heard. They want to be listened to and feel as if the listener really cares about their concerns. Think about it. Have you ever expressed to a friend a problem and in the middle of explaining your dilemma, your friend looks like they are off in Wonderland and couldn't care less about what you are saying? Well if you have been in a situation like this before, you probably know that it is very frustrating not to be listened to. I would even venture to say that your best friend is also probably your greatest listener. This is a wonderful quality to have as a missionary and as a person. Listen to your investigators.

—Understand that all roads lead back to the Book of Mormon: Pearson's book, *The Book of Mormon: Key to Conversion,* expresses rather clearly what an effective conversion tool the Book of Mormon is. No matter what the doubt is, it can be solved by your investigator's knowledge that the Book of Mormon is true. This principle goes back to the point made earlier that the first discussion is much like a chain. The most important link in this chain is the Book of Mormon. It clears up all doubts about any latter-day doctrine that the Church may have. For example, if you have to resolve a concern about polygamy, the Book of Mormon has the answer. Because of polygamy, many people question as to how Joseph Smith could have been a prophet. The answer here is simple. Joseph translated the Book of Mormon. If that book really is of God and his prophets, then there is no way that a false prophet could have translated the golden plates. Therefore, this prophet of God could have in no way introduced a false doctrine to the church after having received the Lord's authority to reestablish his church, starting with the translation of the Book of Mormon. Whenever I was confronted with a doubt like polygamy, I did not spend time in giving reasons of why the Lord might command such a practice. I would only bring the discussion back to the Book of Mormon and point out that if we have a testimony of that book, then we can know that Joseph Smith was given such a revelation. I would recommend Pearson's book. It is a quick read and it will help you to see that the Book of Mormon can clear up any and all doubts.

—Teach so well that there are no doubts: This ability takes much time and practice, but you will find that as you become a better teacher of the gospel, your investigators will have fewer doubts. One example of this was mentioned earlier when I was dealing with the second discussion and baptism. Before you ask someone to be baptized, it is very helpful to explain to him what he will go through before his baptism and the fact that only he will make the final decision. This feeling of empowerment is a great way to help your investigator to relax, set a date, and look forward to his baptism.

—Suggest possible doubts when necessary: Often, when investigators say that they have no doubts, even though it is evident that they do, it is a great idea for you to suggest some possible doubts that your investigator may be having. If I thought that one of my investigators was worried about what his or her family would think if he got baptized, I would mention that one of my main worries before getting baptized was what the reaction of my family would be. Just by pointing out that I had this problem, many investigators would then admit that they were having such doubts and worries.

—Keep the conversation on the main subject: This habit is very important to your success as a teacher. Sometimes, doubts will have a domino effect and just trying to give an answer to a question that you are not really sure of or that is off the beaten path can cause a disruption in the spiritual flow of the discussion. If you see that you are getting too off the subject, make sure that you get back on path quickly. For example, the other night when I went out with the missionaries, we had a nice conversation with two investigators about how they could know if the Book of Mormon was true. After our conversation, they started to ask a barrage of other questions about the Church. We answered a few of their questions, but quickly I reverted back to the main point of our conversation, which was the Book of Mormon. I informed them that all of their other questions would be answered in due time via the discussions, but for now they needed to establish a base, which was a testimony of the Book of Mormon, and therefore a testimony of the Prophet Joseph Smith. By leaving them on that note, I knew that their focus of thought after we left would not be on all of those other questions, but about finding out if what we had taught was true.

—Always stay relaxed when dealing with doubts and concerns: This will instill confidence in your investigators through your example. If they see that you are shaken, then they will also be shaken. If you lack faith, then they will lack faith. I remember that one time an investigator of mine, the night before his baptism, was contemplating not getting baptized. This man's wife and children were strong members and I could tell that the wife was deeply distressed and had given up hope that her husband would be baptized. When the husband told me that he wasn't really sure of his decision and that he thought he wanted to wait, I did not panic, nor did I show any signs of worry. I looked him square in the eyes and told him that I believed in him and that I knew that he would make the right decision. In other words, I made sure he realized just how much faith I had in him and that I knew that if he did get baptized, then he would make a wonderful member. All he needed was for others to feel confident in him as a member. He was baptized the next day and is still active.

—If you don't know the answer, "don't shoot from the hip": I have never had a problem using the words "I don't know." I think some missionaries feel that they have to know everything, but this is not true. Like I said earlier, all they really need is a testimony in the restored gospel and in the Book of Mormon. If your focus is always on the basic truths of the gospel, then the rest of the doubts will take care of themselves over time.

I have not listed in this chapter all of the skills that one must have in order to resolve all doubts and concerns, but what I have listed I know to be very important, as well as true. Just like all other missionary skills, the ability to resolve concerns takes time and effort, but it is well worth any amount of energy you put into it. Start practicing these skills today!

Chapter Fifteen:

Knocking on Doors and Street Contacts

Success consists of going from failure to failure without loss of enthusiasm.
— *Winston Churchill*

There is something about doing street contacts and tracting (knocking doors) as a missionary that just gets me fired up when I think about it. I just loved talking to people about the gospel. I did not always experience great success with the use of these two methods, but at least they enabled me to bear my testimony and feel like a real messenger of Christ, like Alma and Ammon of the Book of Mormon. I have talked with many ex-missionaries who did very little door-knocking on their missions and I have also talked with others who spent most of their time doing so. The purpose of this chapter is not to influence you as a missionary to knock doors all day, which is usually the least effective of all "find" techniques, but rather to help you as a missionary to be successful in your techniques which will lead to effective and worthwhile efforts in the door-knocking approaches and street contacts that you attempt.

There are many ways in which you will find investigators. Your mission president will give you much counsel as to where your focus needs to be to accomplish this task. Personally, I feel that the best way to find new people to teach is to use a variety of methods, which includes working through members, referrals, teaching part-member families, and tracting. I experienced great success with all of these methods in my mission, and that is why I would admonish you to do the same.

It is fun and adventuresome to do a variety of things to find the chosen people in your areas. Tracting, without a doubt, can truly be a rewarding and enjoyable experience every time you and your companion attempt to go out and boldly preach and teach the souls of your designated area. A mission is, or at least it should be, an enjoyable experience, and the crazy, spiritual, humorous, and frustrating experiences that you will have as you tract will be highlights of this great time period.

For the first four months of my mission, I did very little knocking on doors as well as street contacting. I had quite a fear of talking to people in the street or at their doorstep because I feared getting stuck in the middle of a sentence. I would get flustered rather easily and I began to shun away from any opportunity to talk to a stranger spontaneously. I would always leave it up to my senior companion to talk to anyone in the street or on a doorstep.

In the fifth month of my mission, I was given a companion who was well-known in the mission for his interest in knocking on doors. His mission was coming to an end and he had been able to experience much success in regards to finding and baptizing people through tracting. The first couple of times that we went out in our area to work, he wanted to knock doors. I had a negative outlook on his methods, mainly because I had convinced myself that the only way to find good investigators was to work through members. Like many missionaries, I was closed-minded to anything new, but I would soon overcome this pride factor. As we tracted our first night together, my companion asked me to do some of the door approaches. I was hesitant, mainly because of my fear of messing up and saying the wrong thing or not saying anything at all. I did not want to make a fool of myself. With the second door that I knocked on, after a few sentences, I completely bombed out on what I was trying to say. I looked at my companion for help, but he offered very little. I wanted him to back me up, but he knew that I needed to be dependent on my own abilities as a missionary and not on his. I eventually made it through what I wanted to say, and although we did not get in the door, and although I was frustrated with my companion for having left me hanging, I eventually realized that what my companion had me do was of great benefit to my future success as a missionary. He helped me to confront and conquer my fears. From that point on in my mission, I realized that the best way to confront any fear that you may have in your mission, or even in your life, is to take it head-on.

I once heard a talk on fear which included the fact that when cows are in a field and there is a storm coming, they all line up together in one single file line and face directly into the storm. As missionaries, we must do the same and face all problems and difficulties head on. If we are afraid to knock on doors, we must practice it until it becomes fun, easy, and exciting. This is also true with regards to bearing our testimonies, challenging someone to baptism, or any other commitment for that matter. Such practice can be accomplished not only while tracting in your proselyting areas, but also within the walls of your apartment. Just practicing a variety of situations with your companion can lead to an amazing amount of improvement and confidence on your part. Fear is only in the mind. You have the ability to be a fearless missionary. Commit yourself to being such, and then work and pray to accomplish your goal.

As I have already mentioned, I grew to enjoy tracting as time went on in my mission. I just loved seeing how many people I could talk with as each day flew by. As I progressed, I realized that there were many helpful techniques for door approaches as well as contacts. It is a funny fact that some people have wonderful success in regards to finding people through tracting, whereas others, who spend just as much time attempting to find investigators through such techniques, have very little success. Why is this? Well the answer is simple. It has to do with your ability to light a fire in the eyes and hearts of the people you come in contact with. They must see in you something that they have not seen before. They must take from you a feeling that they have never experienced. You have such a power. Of course, this is not possible with everyone that you come in contact with as a missionary, but it can be a fairly common occurrence. Any missionary can have success through tracting if they just do and say the right things. A few suggestions to help you to unlock your tracting potential include:

—Practice a great deal. Once again, I must emphasize the need to practice your skills with your companion and the other missionaries in your zone or district. Role-playing activities can be extremely helpful if the participants are humble and willing to learn.

—Make it fun and get excited! Tracting does not have to be a drag! It all depends on the attitude of the missionaries. If you jog from house to house and have a smile of joy and enthusiasm on your face the whole time you are doing it, people will be so taken by your energy that they will be waiting for you to stop by their houses and give them some of your happiness. Believe me, I have seen this happen countless times, because there are so many people in the world that just have not experienced true happiness in their lives. These people are waiting for someone to boost them up and give them a reason for existence. You are that person! Get fired up before you go out knocking doors and you will see the benefits, and when success does not occur immediately, get even more enthusiastic and eventually, your persistence will pay off.

—Do not use the same-door or contact approach every time. How can you possibly expect people to want to hear your message if they see no fire in your eyes? If a missionary says the same thing at the door every time, they will sound robotic and people see right through that. Get creative! Try not to say the same thing twice in a row. Let the Spirit, as well as your enthusiastic personality, say the words for you.

So many of the people that you will come in contact with out there in the world have already been approached by Latter-day Saint missionaries in the past. Most of these missionaries have said the same thing. Don't allow yourself to continue the lethargic chain of "Hi, we are missionaries from the Church of Jesus Christ of Latter-day Saints and we have a message about the plan of our Heavenly Father."

Now don't get me wrong, I am not saying that mentioning the plan of our Heavenly Father is wrong, but don't you think that something like this would be more effective:

"Hello, there! My name is Elder Sheridan and I am so excited to be here in Chile talking to you this day. You may wonder why I am so excited. It is because I have been given the chance to come to this wonderful country for two years, leave my other life behind, and talk to the loving people of this country about our Heavenly Father's plan."

Can you see the difference between the two approaches? On the first approach, little enthusiasm was shown and the missionary got right to the point without setting a mood for the potential investigator. In the second approach, the missionary was loaded with enthusiasm and he did two very important things: One, he complimented the country in which he was located and, two, he complimented the people of that country. Just by doing this, the listener feels a sense of pride. After having received such a compliment, it is much less likely that a person will be rude to the missionary. In fact, the potential investigator is more likely to want to live up to that billing and be friendly to the two young men in white shirts and ties. Another important element of the second approach was the fact that the missionary talked a little about himself and what he was doing, thus opening up a little. You will see that many people out there are very curious about Mormon missionaries. Whenever I would use such an approach in my mission, I would often get a return comment of " Was it hard to leave your other life behind" or " Do you miss your family?" Questions like these are very helpful in breaking the ice with a non-member. The more the non-member asks questions about you and your life, the more opportunities you will have to bear your testimony, teach, and build relationships of trust with that person.

—Make them laugh. Is there one person in this world who doesn't enjoy laughing? If there is, I have yet to meet him. Laughing has so much power, and your ability to make your investigators smile and laugh will be of great help to you in building relationships of trust and helping your investigators to feel relaxed when they are with you. I am not trying to say that you should not have a spirit of reverence as a missionary, but I am saying that humor definitely has its place among the many conversion tools that you have. If you are at a doorstep, and someone opens the door and is not in a very good mood, it is likely that he will tell you to go away. But, if you knock on someone's door, and he is in a bad mood, and you figure out a way to make them laugh, then your chances of getting in that door have greatly increased. You should start now trying to make your friends and family laugh when they are in bad moods, and then try to talk to them about anything at all. You will quickly see the miraculous results from a simple laugh.

—Give a sincere compliment. Everyone loves to get a compliment. It is just an inherent part of man. No matter where you go in the world, the people in your mission will love your compliments. You must become a master of giving sincere compliments. This attribute will also greatly help you in the real world after your mission. Whenever I would meet someone for the first time on my mission, I would always look for a compliment to give that person. For example, if you are going to a part-member family's house for dinner, and the father of the household is not a member, it is a great idea that, to break the ice with this man, you give him some type of compliment. An example of this could be telling him how impressed you are with the number of livestock he has on his farm or congratulate him on the soccer trophies that he has collected over the years. Just by doing this, you have lit a fire of enthusiasm in the father and given him the chance to talk about himself and his accolades. If you just sit there for a while and listen to him talk about what he has accomplished in his life or what he deals with on a day-to-day basis, he will be much more apt to sit down and listen to you talk about the Plan of Salvation. On the other hand, if you try to shove the message of the Church down his throat as soon as you meet him, he will probably turn you off pretty fast.

In regard to giving compliments or saying something positive, I would stress that it is a must that you are honest in your praise and approval. Don't say kind things just so you will have a better chance of teaching a discussion. This is called flattery and it does not work. Be kind because you want to be kind. Give honest compliments because you want that other person to feel good about him or herself. You must be a friend to all if you want to taste the fruits of successful missionary work.

—Don't just talk, listen. Too many missionaries are so wrapped up in what they are trying to say that they never truly hear what an investigator is saying. If you are making a street contact, and someone starts to tell you a little about him—or herself, give him the chance. If you do not, he will not be interested in listening to you.

—Let the Spirit guide you. I talk a lot about temporal techniques and methods in this book, which, as I have explained, are necessary. But don't forget that you must do everything in your mission with the guidance of the Spirit. Pray for help as to whom to talk to and where you should knock doors. Let the Spirit guide you in all of the conversations that you may have as a missionary. The ability and gift to use the Spirit is the greatest "technique" of all those that are listed in this book.

—Set "real" appointments. If you knock on a door and someone tells you to come back another time, be sure that you give them a choice of two times in which you can return to their home. If you ask them when you can return without giving any time frame, they are likely to tell you to come back in a few weeks which, needless to say, is very ineffective. You need to return to their homes within a few days. Also, if you plan with someone a certain time to return to their house, give them a written reminder telling them when you plan to return. This simple act will only take a few seconds, but it is sure to save you from being "dogged" as much by your investigators.

—No wild goose chases. When doing a street contact, it is always necessary to know exactly what the person's address is with whom you plan to make a visit. One major problem with street contacts is the fact that many people will welcome you to their house but give you a false address. There is nothing more frustrating than looking for a house that does not exist. When a person tells you his address, have them repeat it to you twice during the conversation. Although this will not guarantee that you are not given the wrong address, it will key you in to whenever a person is not telling the truth, mainly because he will often make an error the second time he tells you where he lives. Also, make sure you get a good description of the person's house whenever making a contact.

—Don't give up! I promise you that you will face much rejection as you go about knocking doors and talking to people in the street. It is one of those difficult parts of your service that cannot be escaped. You must accept this fact and realize that with the bad, much good will also come about. Don't get depressed! Satan wants you to do just that. Promise yourself that you will have an energy and pep to your walk and talk every time you tract. Believe in yourself and the results will follow.

I could probably give a hundred more tips on how to tract more effectively, but just as I have pointed out many times in this book, you should exercise your creative powers so that you can see what works best for you. Just as you must develop your abilities to teach the discussions, it is crucial to your success and happiness that you develop your skills in tracting.

I testify that there are many people out there who are just waiting for you to come up to them on the street, make them smile, and then share a message with them that will change their lives forever. Some of the greatest converts in my mission come from tracting efforts. I do not want you to think that I am recommending in this chapter that one should tract all day long and not worry about working through the members to find investigators, but if you do use tracting methods to find investigators in your mission, you can be very successful if you go about it with a relentless enthusiasm along with the help of the Holy Ghost.

I would also suggest that you try as many different methods as possible to find new investigators. For example, in some areas I did very little tracting because I was able to find and baptize through the use of the members. In other areas, where I had difficulty working through the members, I was very successful in finding investigators through tracting. This is why it is so important to be skilled in as many "find" methods as possible.

Some of my happiest times in the mission came when I was outside in the pouring rain and wind, going from door to door as the rain and wind slapped my face, sharing something that meant everything to me—the gospel of Jesus Christ. During such times, I was able to feel the closest to the Savior. I will cherish those simple memories for the rest of eternity.

Chapter Sixteen:

It's All About Attitude

A pessimist sees the difficulty in every opportunity, an optimist sees the opportunity in every difficulty.
—Winston Churchill

You may have heard that serving a mission will help you to learn who you really are. This is absolutely true. The funny thing is, though, that whether it be in life or in the mission, we do not usually "find ourselves" when everything is fine and dandy. To the contrary, you will most likely find out who you really are once you are faced with adversity. Adversity is an undeniable aspect of a mission, but it is also a very important aspect. It is what makes us grow and prepares us to be husbands, fathers, mothers, and leaders. It is the chisel that shapes and forms us into spiritual rocks. It is a requisite of our spiritual progress.

It is easy for any missionary to be happy when they are in a great area with great members. It is easy for any missionary to be happy when they are baptizing often and reaching all of their goals, and it is easy to be transferred to an area that always baptizes. In circumstances like these, attitude and optimism are usually very high, as you can imagine.

Now I would like to do a little exercise. I am going give you a scenario, and I want you to imagine that you really are in that situation. How would you honestly react if you found yourself in one of these situations:

—You are very obedient and hardworking. Despite this fact, you have not had a baptism in three months.

—You are set to have a family of five get baptized after church. You have been working toward this day for months. All of the members are excited for you and your companion, as well as for the family. Everyone is coming to the baptism. It is your "golden family." Your emotions are riding high. Once church begins, the family is not there and it appears that they have changed their minds.

—You are in a great area. You and your companion have exceeded all of your goals in the two months that you have been there. The mission president calls you out of the blue and says that he needs you to transfer to an area in the mission that is notorious because no missionary has had a baptism there in fifteen months. You can't believe the news, especially since you are were "on a roll" in your current location.

—You have been knocking doors for an hour in the rain. You are freezing and everyone that you have talked to has been rude and impatient. You feel that it may be better to just go to your apartment early.

—Your girlfriend of five years dumps you just two weeks before you are about to go home. You are shocked and baffled. Do you go into a depression or finish with a bang?

These are just a few of the obstacles that I have seen missionaries deal with. What would be your reaction to these events? Do you rise to the occasion or do you forget who you are and let Satan bring you down with him. If you do find yourself in a situation comparable to one of these in the mission field, that is when you will find the "true" you. That is also when you will build your character and conquer Satan's temptations.

I had many experiences like the ones mentioned. In some occasions, I acted rather valiantly. In other occasions, I could have done much better. I would like to share with you an experience that helped to make me the person that I am today.

I had been out a little over three months in the mission field. I was still struggling with the language and my companion and I had just finished off a month where we had baptized no one. Despite our lack of initial success, we had found a great family and they were progressing quite well and were going to be baptized that month if all went as planned.

On the first Sunday of the month, we finally had a baptism scheduled, which would take place in the evening. The lady's name was Katty and she was one of the members of this important family that we had in our teaching pool. We knew that if things went well with her baptism, then her family would most likely follow in her footsteps. After church, we filled up the font and looked forward to the beginning of what we hoped would be a fruitful month. Finally, at 7:00 that night, everything was set. Katty looked great and was excited for her new beginning. We all went to the baptismal room where there were about forty people, ten of whom were investigators. My companion and I had about seven investigators there and the sister missionaries had about three. We were all very excited and wanted to ensure that everything went well so that the Spirit could help all of the investigators to progress. With everyone seated and Katty ready to enter into the font, I began to open the sliding curtain in front of the font so that everyone could witness the special occasion. Then, all of a sudden, my stomach shot up in my throat and a surge of worry soared throughout my body. The font was empty! I was shocked. What were we going to do?

As soon as my companion and the sisters saw what was going on, everyone started to panic. Someone had apparently pulled the plug in the font and it would take at least forty five minutes to fill it up with cold water. (It normally takes about three hours with hot water, but we knew that three hours was way too long). At this point, we had two options: One, we could postpone the baptism to a later date, but that would seriously compromise Katty's situation as well as affect the rest of the investigators that were there. Or two, we could do something else for about an hour which would give us enough time to fill the font up and therefore complete the baptism. As the four of us missionaries talked, we decided to that our only possible choice would be to do some sort of activity for an hour while the font was filling.

After coming up with this conclusion, the three other missionaries looked at me. I got scared. I knew that they wanted me to come up with the activity. The thought came to me that "I'm the one who can't even speak the language well." Despite the negative thoughts that came to my mind, I gritted my teeth and decided to face my fears head on. I also knew that up to that point in my mission I had not achieved my potential because my fears had gotten in the way, and so I was not about to let myself down again.

The next action I took was to call everyone into the chapel. I informed them that we were having problems with the font and that we needed a little bit of time to fix it. Then I stood in front of those forty or so people and began to lead a spiritual conversation based on the first discussion. The room quickly filled with the Spirit and I could even feel my nervousness turn into confidence and excitement. Before long, everyone in the chapel was sharing their testimony of the principles that I was teaching. Investigators were also participating, asking questions and even bearing their own testimonies of the things the missionaries had taught them. It was thrilling! The members were very excited to help and it was almost as if the spirit in the room was going back and forth, bouncing off of everyone that was in the room. I could hardly believe what was taking place. Before I knew it, the font had been filled, and the baptism turned out great!

The rest of Katty's family was also baptized that month. I owe this mainly to the feelings that we all shared that night in the chapel. After having had such a strong spiritual experience, the rest of the family wanted to taste such joy for themselves.

On a side note, one funny thing that was said to me that night was a comment from the bishop's wife. She told me that during the fireside in the chapel, I "was completely dominating of the language as well as the audience." What she said made me feel great, mainly because she liked to hassle me for not speaking the language well. It also made me realize that the gift of tongues does exist; it just takes certain circumstances for Heavenly Father to help us to go beyond our normal abilities.

My experience with the empty baptismal font taught me that in the mission, as well as in life, there are going to be some very tight and nerve-racking moments. One can either step up to the challenge and see the "opportunity in the difficulty," or they can give up. Shakespeare once said, "There is no such thing as good or bad, but thinking makes it so." I think that this is a great quote. It is so very applicable to the mission field. Your attitude will dictate your success, as well as your personal conversion, during your time as a missionary. Do not fall into the trap of letting the opinions of others dictate your opinions and actions. If someone tells you that you are going to the "worst" area in the mission, reply to that person that you plan on making it the best, and then do so. If you feel like you are having one of those days where you just keep getting rejected and nothing goes right, stick your chin a little higher in the air and smile a little brighter. In such moments of resilience do the greatest of all miracles occur. Let no one define who you are as a missionary or the success that you will have. *You* define yourself as well your success.

I know that if you have the right attitude and rise to the occasion when all else seems to go wrong in the mission, you will develop into a person that you had never previously imagined. You will achieve greatness in every aspect of life, it just take a determination and a never-say-never attitude. Unleash you greatness and, as Emerson said, "Hitch your wagon to a star!"

Chapter Seventeen:

Goals and Numbers

Earlier in the book, I mentioned that goals and numbers were a very important aspect of the mission field, as well as life. For the next two years or eighteen months of your life, every day you will be setting goals and trying to reach certain numbers. You have two choices with regards to goals and numbers. You can love them, or you can despise them. The purpose of writing this chapter is to help you to realize that goals and numbers are a very important and needed aspect of the mission field, and without them you cannot reach your potential.

President Hinckley set the goal to have more than 100 temples in operation by the year 2000, a goal that he accomplished. Just by reviewing this stat, we can safely say that the prophet feels that goals and numbers are very important. I would also venture to say that when the Prophet made such a bold statement, he intended to do everything possible to reach such a lofty goal.

As missionaries we must do the same thing. We must take our goals seriously. Often, I think that we do not take our goals seriously because we do not understand what they really are. Goals, when set properly through prayer and study, are covenants that we make with our Father in Heaven. The key word here is *covenant*.

The Bible Dictionary tells us that a covenant is "an agreement between two persons; more often between God and man; but in this latter case it is important to notice that the two parties to the agreement do not stand in the relation of independent and equal contractors. God in his good pleasure fixes the terms, which man accepts... The gospel is so arranged that principles and ordinances are received by covenant placing the recipient under strong obligation and responsibility to honor the commitment..."

As you set your goals in the mission field, start off with prayer. You must have the direction of our Father in Heaven to really know your potential as well as the potential of your area. Notice that the definition says that God fixes the terms. This is very important. Let's say that you and your companion are having an inventory meeting and there are three people in your teaching pool that you feel will probably get baptized that month. Upon praying about your baptismal goal for the month, you both are surprised to find that you feel there are *six*, and not just three, people in the area that have been prepared to accept the gospel. Six, therefore, would probably be a good goal for your companionship to set for the month, even though you do not yet have all of those people in your teaching pool. Now, after having set your goal at six baptisms, do everything possible to ensure that this goal is reached, and as the previous definition says, you have accepted the strong obligation and responsibility to honor the commitment.

Recently, I talked to one of the missionaries that I trained in the mission field. His name is Brandon Smith and he had been home for a few weeks when we talked. The last few months of his mission were spent in the office as an assistant and he had really helped to set the mission on fire. Baptisms had almost doubled. I asked him what the key to their success was and he told me that the missionaries finally started to take their covenants (goals) with Heavenly Father seriously. He said that this was very difficult at first, mainly because some missionaries were very timid and pessimistic about making such a commitment. It was so impressive and inspiring to hear his testimony on the matter. He said that he had never felt so close to the Savior than when he was sincerely and earnestly striving to reach the covenants that he had made. He also said that the mission had become much more consecrated and focused, mainly because everyone had the same vision. Because I had not talked with Elder Brandon Smith for more than a year, I was in awe of the testimony that he had gained during his service to the Savior. He had spiritually progressed beyond my wildest dreams. Just listening to his sincere words made me want to be a better person and draw closer to the Lord.

We can learn a lot from the example of Brandon Smith. He took his goals seriously, never made excuses for not reaching them, and understood their importance. Through his example and success, many other missionaries also were able to taste the fruits of accepting the covenants that our Heavenly Father has given us. I know that we all can do this. Numbers and goals are not to be taken lightly. They really are promises with the Lord and through these promises I testify in the name of Jesus Christ that we will form a relationship and communion with the Father and the Son that we had never previously imagined possible.

Chapter Eighteen:

Exercise

In Chapter Two, I talked somewhat about the importance of exercise while out in the mission field. We have also already established the fact that your mission will develop the habits that you have for the rest of your life. I have written this chapter to reiterate a very important point. Exercise is a crucial aspect of your physical and mental well-being as a person! You have taken the time to read this book to ensure yourself that you can be the best preacher of the gospel possible. If you truly have such a desire, then you will undoubtedly want to do the little things that will guarantee results. Exercise is one of those little things.

Before I give some basic ideas on what you can do to get exercise while in the field, I first want to point out that exercise should never be a priority in your mission, nor should it impede your abilities to convert people to the gospel. Anyone who works out for an hour each day in their pre-mission life must simply accept the fact that they are not going to be able to keep up those habits during the mission. We are not called on missions in order to look more like Arnold Schwarzenegger; but—and I want to stress this point—fitness can be maintained in the mission field. All it takes, just like any other success-inducing habit, is planning, goal setting, and follow-through. I will give my own personal example:

All of my friends knew that I was a fitness geek before I left on my mission. Many of these friends had already gone on missions, and some of them had come back looking much larger than when they had started their missions. When I would tell my friends that I planned on keeping fit and doing exercise while out in the mission field, they would normally chuckle and say something like, "Everyone says that, but no one ever does. You'll see." Such statements really aggravated me. I thought to myself that just because they were too lazy to do fifteen minutes of exercise a day did not mean that I would follow in their footsteps. To prove my friends wrong, I told them that I would do pushups and situps every day of my mission (except on Sundays), and I would even record in a journal all that I was able to do. (I later found that keeping a written record helped me to stay motivated.)

Since I had committed myself to exercise and wasn't about to let my friends get the best of me, I started my good habits on day one in the MTC and kept them up until my last day in the mission field. Every six months or so, I would send a letter back to my college ward informing everyone about my mission, but also where I stood on my "exercise count." I would sometimes even get letters from my friends asking me how high my count had gotten. It was rather funny and a good laugh for everyone. Finally by the end of my mission, I was able to look back in my exercise journal and count everything that I had done. These were the results:

—82,434 push-ups
—227,902 sit-ups
—342,750 jumping jacks
—250 miles ran
—1310 floors climbed (In my last area we lived in a twelve-story building.)
—155 minutes of jumping rope

Now please don't think that I have printed these numbers because I want everyone to think that I have done something wonderful. I just want you to see what fifteen to twenty minutes of exercise a day can add up to during a two-year time period. Upon my arrival home, I went back to those friends who had doubted me and pointed out to them what I had accomplished. It felt good to prove that I could be motivated enough to get some type of exercise every day, but more than anything, these exercises really helped my performance as a missionary. I have included a few of the benefits of exercise that I found while I was in the mission field:

Exercise keeps your enthusiasm up, especially in the morning. For many missionaries, it is very difficult to study in the morning. But if you jump out of your bed every morning and do jumping jacks or run in place for ten minutes, and then take a shower, you will find that you are absolutely alert during your morning study period. I have always found that I just feel so much more enthused after a good workout. My confidence is better and my will to do is stronger. Exercise does wonders with the mind.

Exercise keeps you from turning into a chunk. Be honest, do you want to be one of those missionaries who comes home twenty five pounds heavier and is not even recognized by his family as he gets off the plane? Of course not! The two ways to prevent this are to have a good diet and to exercise. Look at it this way: If you do fifteen minutes of exercise a day, six days a week, that adds up to ninety minutes of exercise a week. Ninety minutes of light aerobic exercise will burn about one thousand or more calories. Therefore, every month you burn off at least one pound of fat (one pound of fat equals 3600 calories), which in turn means that you burn off at least twelve pounds of fat in a year or twenty four pounds of fat in two years! Now can you see why missionaries come home twenty five pounds heavier? They just won't take the time to get 15 minutes of exercise a day. It is that simple.

Exercise gives you a release from stress. A mission can be very stressful, and exercise can be your means of clearing your head, relaxing, and finding answers that you had previously not thought of.

Exercise will keep you awake. Whether it is done in the morning, afternoon, or evening, exercise will get the blood pumping and wake up the whole body. I would always do jumping jacks in the morning to help me with my studies and then I would do sit-ups and pushups in the afternoon after lunch to keep me from falling asleep. I found that exercising gave me a much better boost than a nap ever did. Try it for yourself and you will understand what I am saying.

I hope that you are now committed to going out and getting yourself an exercise journal so that you can keep track of all the exercise that you do during the next two years or eighteen months. I have a very strong testimony of the need to stay physically fit while out in the mission field. Don't let your body wilt away while you serve. Make the commitment and you will see just how great the results can be.

Chapter Nineteen:

Running Through the Finish Line

"Trunky" is one of the most commonly used slang terms in the mission field. I would also say that it is one of the most disheartening words, mainly because it describes a missionary who gets lazy during his final months of the mission. Trunkiness is a sad aspect of every mission, but your example can help others to keep going hard until the end of their appointed days.

No matter how great a missionary you are during your time out in the field, you will always be remembered by your fellow missionaries by the last impressions that you leave them. If you decide to sleep in the final two months of your mission, you will be remembered as "Elder Sleep." Such should not be your legacy! Do not fall into the trap of laziness and complacency. Slacking off at the end will mar everything that you have worked so hard to accomplish during your time as a missionary. It will rip away at the spiritual shield that you have developed over the past two years.

Because I love running, I look at the mission as if it were a race. The goal of any runner is to run every race with all of his mental and physical strength, thus pushing himself to the edge. Only upon doing this can one really feel a sense of accomplishment. One of the best feelings in the world is sprinting the final leg of a race, feeling your legs burn and heart race as you grit your way through the finish line, then collapse as you have finally reached your goal. You can have this same feeling in your mission. You have the ability to go out with a bang. I feel that I was able to finish my mission on a sprint; and that feeling of lasting to the end, even though I was tempted to slow down, is one of the great highlights of my missionary experience.

It is now your turn to run such a race, and the best thing is that you are only competing against yourself. The pace that you will set is up to you. Whether you run or crawl through the finish line is your decision. Your potential is endless. As for you final months in the mission field, I will leave you with this quote by Warren Zevon: "I will sleep when I am dead."

Chapter Twenty:

Sitting on the Fence

I hope that you have enjoyed reading the information found within these pages. I have loved writing this book. It has helped me quite a bit in many ways. It has given me the opportunity to reflect on the greatest two years of my life. As I close, I would like to hit on one last point:

The life of a missionary is full of decision-making. Everyday, you will have to decide to wake up on time or not, to study or not, to say your prayers or not, to leave to work on time or not, and to work yourself in the ground or not, among others. As you can see, there are many, many decisions that you will have to make as a missionary. Your ability to make decisions can be greatly enhanced as you serve your Lord and Redeemer. As you follow the promptings of the Spirit and make the right decisions during your service, you will grow more and more confident in your decision-making abilities. You will develop a bond with your Father in Heaven that you have never had before.

The thing about decisions though, especially in regards to the gospel, is that there is nothing worse than indecision. We must decide to act as missionaries. We must commit ourselves to success, no matter what the odds are against us. We must do what is right and only then can we realize just who we are in terms of our relationship with Heavenly Father. Yes, your mission will enable you to know just who you are.

I was able to read the incredible book *Jesus the Christ* by James Talmage, while out in the mission field. It touched me like no book ever has. One particular passage of the book struck me harder than any other aspect of it. In the first chapter, Talmage explains rather in depth the pre-existence and the war that took place in Heaven before we all came to earth. As you have probably studied before, two-thirds of the hosts of Heaven followed the Savior's plan while the other one-third followed the plan of Lucifer. During this debate, you and I had to decide with whom we would side with. Luckily, we chose the plan of our elder brother, and could therefore come to Earth and receive a body.

Despite this fact, Talmage points out that two-thirds of the spirit children either fought on the side of Jesus Christ or, "at least did not actively oppose our brother's plan." This particular statement by Talmage struck me deeply when I first read it. It made me realize that some of us were front-line fighters, while others of us were simple fence-sitters. I read this statement about halfway through my mission and for the rest of my mission, I wondered and thought about what I had done during my pre-earthly years. Did I fight or did I sit?

On the final day of my mission, my fellow missionaries and I sat in a nice chartered bus for twelve hours from Osorno to Santiago where everyone would catch their planes for home. The bus ride was a time of great contemplation as well as excitement for all of us. Our time had come and gone, and it was like an amazing dream for everyone. With so much time to reflect, I brought my thoughts back to Talmage's book and the idea of fighting or sitting the fence. At that moment of contemplation and reflection, I felt an overwhelming sense of joy and accomplishment. That was my answer! I had fought! My mission showed me that I was willing to stand up for what I believed and confront fear and doubts with my chin held high. I also realized that I was going to fight for the cause of the Lord for the rest of my life. A new mission was about to begin.

You, too, will be able to find out what your pre-earth

actions were as you serve a mission for the Church of Jesus Christ of Latter-day Saints. You will learn your strengths and your weaknesses. You will find out the type of person you want to strive to be and you will also find out what type of person you want to spend the rest of your life with.

Now here is the charge: Go out and serve. Work your hardest and find what true happiness is. Learn to make decisions and catch a glimpse of your place in the grand scheme of things. Your time has come. You will now be one of Heavenly Father's Angels, this I say in the name of Jesus Christ, Amen.

About the Author

Marcus Sheridan

Marcus Edward Sheridan was born in North Carolina on November 6, 1977, and spent most of his growing years living in Eastern Virginia along the Chesapeake Bay, in the small town of Callao. It was not until his senior year that Sheridan was introduced to the missionaries and baptized into the Church of Jesus Christ of Latter-day Saints, during which time he was the only active male member of his high school.

After graduation, Sheridan moved on to the mountainous region of Morgantown, West Virginia, where he attended college at West Virginia University. While working with the missionaries in Morgantown, as well as while participating with other single adults, his testimony reached a point where he knew and understood the importance of serving a mission.

Marcus Sheridan was called to serve in the Osorno, Chile mission from 1997 to 1999. He excelled as a missionary and became known throughout the mission for his enthusiasm, work ethic, and use of original teaching methods.

Thomas Lyon, a BYU professor and Sheridan's mission president said, "Of all the missionaries that I worked with during my three-year term, Marcus showed more ability to innovate and motivate than any other. Marcus demonstrates the fine ability to be creative at the same time he is perfectly obedient to mission structure and Church policies—a rare gift among missionaries. He continues to carry out this disciplined, innovative approach to life and missionary work."

Upon completion of his mission, Sheridan married his longtime sweetheart, Nichole Hayden, and has since had a child while completing his studies in college. He has become well-known throughout Northern West Virginia for his motivational talks for the youth and his enthusiasm for sharing the gospel.

CEDAR FORT, INCORPORATED
Order Form

Name:_____

Address: _____

City: _____ State: _____ Zip: _____

Phone: (   ) _____ Daytime phone: (   ) _____

Heavenly Father's Angels

Quantity: _____ @ $12.95 each: _____

plus $3.49 shipping & handling for the first book: _____

(add 99¢ shipping for each additional book)

Utah residents add 6.25% for state sales tax: _____

TOTAL: _____

Bulk purchasing, shipping and handling quotes available upon request.

Please make check or money order payable to:
Cedar Fort, Incorporated.

Mail this form and payment to:
Cedar Fort, Inc.
925 North Main St.
Springville, UT 84663

You can also order on our website **www.cedarfort.com**
or e-mail us at sales@cedarfort.com or call 1-800-SKYBOOK